Crime & Justice

Editor: Danielle Lobban

Volume 437

independence
educational publishers

Acknowledgements

The publisher is grateful for permission to reproduce the material in this book. While every care has been taken to trace and acknowledge copyright, the publisher tenders its apology for any accidental infringement or where copyright has proved untraceable. The publisher would be pleased to come to a suitable arrangement in any such case with the rightful owner.

The material reproduced in **issues** books is provided as an educational resource only. The views, opinions and information contained within reprinted material in **issues** books do not necessarily represent those of Independence Educational Publishers and its employees.

Images

Cover image courtesy of iStock. All other images courtesy of Freepik, Pixabay and Unsplash.

Additional acknowledgements

With thanks to the Independence team: Shelley Baldry, Tracy Biram, Klaudia Sommer and Jackie Staines.

Danielle Lobban

Cambridge, January 2024

Contents

Introduction

Crime & Justice is Volume 437 in the **issues** series. The aim of the series is to offer current, diverse information about important issues in our world, from a UK perspective.

About Crime & Justice

After a decade of a drop in crime, there has been a sharp rise in some parts of the UK over the past couple of years. This book looks at how crime is dealt with and the ways to deter and prevent criminal behaviour.

Our sources

Titles in the **issues** series are designed to function as educational resource books, providing a balanced overview of a specific subject.

The information in our books is comprised of facts, articles and opinions from many different sources, including:

- Newspaper reports and opinion pieces
- Website factsheets
- Magazine and journal articles
- Statistics and surveys
- Government reports
- Literature from special interest groups.

A note on critical evaluation

Because the information reprinted here is from a number of different sources, readers should bear in mind the origin of the text and whether the source is likely to have a particular bias when presenting information (or when conducting their research). It is hoped that, as you read about the many aspects of the issues explored in this book, you will critically evaluate the information presented.

It is important that you decide whether you are being presented with facts or opinions. Does the writer give a biased or unbiased report? If an opinion is being expressed, do you agree with the writer? Is there potential bias to the 'facts' or statistics behind an article?

Activities

Throughout this book, you will find a selection of assignments and activities designed to help you engage with the articles you have been reading and to explore your own opinions. Some tasks will take longer than others and there is a mixture of design, writing and research-based activities that you can complete alone or in a group.

Further research

At the end of each article we have listed its source and a website that you can visit if you would like to conduct your own research. Please remember to critically evaluate any sources that you consult and consider whether the information you are viewing is accurate and unbiased.

Issues Online

The **issues** series of books is complemented by our online resource, issuesonline.co.uk

On the Issues Online website you will find a wealth of information, covering over 70 topics, to support the PSHE and RSE curriculum.

Why Issues Online?

Researching a topic? Issues Online is the best place to start for...

Librarians

Issues Online is an essential tool for librarians: feel confident you are signposting safe, reliable, user-friendly online resources to students and teaching staff alike. We provide multi-user concurrent access, so no waiting around for another student to finish with a resource. Issues Online also provides FREE downloadable posters for your shelf/wall/table displays.

Teachers

Issues Online is an ideal resource for lesson planning, inspiring lively debate in class and setting lessons and homework tasks.

Our accessible, engaging content helps deepen students' knowledge, promotes critical thinking and develops independent learning skills.

Issues Online saves precious preparation time. We wade through the wealth of material on the internet to filter the best quality, most relevant and up-to-date information you need to start exploring a topic.

Our carefully selected, balanced content presents an overview and insight into each topic from a variety of sources and viewpoints.

Students

Issues Online is designed to support your studies in a broad range of topics, particularly social issues relevant to young people today.

Thousands of articles, statistics and infographs instantly available to help you with research and assignments.

With 24/7 access using the powerful Algolia search system, you can find relevant information quickly, easily and safely anytime from your laptop, tablet or smartphone, in class or at home.

Visit issuesonline.co.uk to find out more!

What is crime?

Crime, or behaviour which goes against the criminal law, covers a very wide variety of acts, from the relatively trivial, such as possessing class C drugs, to the very serious, such as murder.

By Karl Thompson

A definition of Crime

A simple, starting point definition of crime is:

Crime – *the term used to describe behaviour which is against the criminal law. Crime is law-breaking behaviour.*

What counts as criminal behaviour thus varies depending on what the laws of a society deem to be illegal. What is legal in one country may not be legal in another.

A closely related concept to crime is deviance which is rule-breaking behaviour which fails to conform to the norms and expectations of a particular society or social group. Criminal behaviour is usually also deviant behaviour, but there is a lot of deviant behaviour which isn't criminal.

This article focuses on the questions of what crime and criminal behaviour are. It has been written primarily as an introduction to the Crime and Deviance module for A-level sociology students.

The social Construction of Crime

Newburn (2007) suggests that crime is basically a label that is attached to certain forms of behaviour which are prohibited by the state (government), and have some legal penalty against them. While crime therefore seems easy to define, as the law states what a criminal act is, there is no act that is criminal in itself. An act only becomes a crime when agents of the state label that act as criminal in a particular context. For example, killing someone with a knife during a fight outside a pub in the UK is a criminal offence, but killing an armed combatant during wartime with a knife is not.

Criminal law also varies from country to country, and criminal law changes over time within one country, which reinforces the idea that there is no such thing as an inherently criminal act.

If we examine how the law differs from country to country, it shows us the extent to which 'crime is socially constructed'.

One example is the variations in the laws surrounding homosexuality – which is punishable by death in 12 countries, but in the United Kingdom and many other European countries it is illegal to discriminate on the basis of sexuality.

A second example is that women in Saudi Arabia are still effectively banned from wearing clothes which 'show off their beauty' (according to an article in *The Week*, January 2020), however this is open to interpretation, and some resistance from women flouting the rules.

Discussion Question: why might the law (and thus the nature and extent of 'crime') vary so much across countries?

The Law in England and Wales

While you don't need an in-depth understanding of the legal system it is useful to know something about it because it will help you understand where the law comes from and thus how the law changes, and consequently how crime changes over time.

There are two main sources of law in England and Wales

- Common Law, which evolves through decisions made by judges at trials, which set precedents for future trials.

- Statute Law, which comes about through an Act of Parliament – typically through bills proposed by members of parliament which are debated and modified, often over several months, which then become acts of law.

The Gradual Evolution of Common Law in England and Wales

English criminal law derives its main principles from common law. The main elements of a crime are the actus reus (doing something which is criminally prohibited) and a mens rea (having the requisite criminal state of mind, usually intention or recklessness). A prosecutor must show that a person has caused the offensive conduct, or that the culprit had some pre-existing duty to take steps to avoid a criminal consequence. The types of different crimes range from those well-known ones like manslaughter, murder, theft and robbery to a plethora of regulatory and statutory offences. Today it is estimated that in the UK, there are 3,500 classes of criminal offence.

Parliamentary Acts and Changes to Law in England and Wales

Over the last two centuries, many new laws have been introduced through over 4500 Acts of Parliament which have responded to various social changes, one of the most recent being the 'Psychoactive Substances Act of 2016 which made it illegal to supply a number of so called 'legal highs'.

One single act can also make a number of behaviours illegal – such as with the 2010 equality act, which made it illegal for employers to discriminate against Transgender people and pregnant women.

NB – The fact that there are so many acts of Parliament demonstrates the extent to which crime is socially constructed. Since 2010 there have been more than 200 new Acts of Parliament.

The main categories of crime in England and Wales

Today, The Crown Prosecution Service recognises eleven classes of criminal offence, ranging from very serious (class A) through to Miscellaneous lesser offences (class I).

- Class A: Homicide and related grave offences. E.g. Murder
- Class B: Offences involving serious violence or damage, and serious drugs offences. E.g. kidnapping, armed robbery.
- Class C: Lesser offences involving violence or damage, and less serious drugs offences – e.g. possession of firearm without certificate.
- Class D: Sexual offences, and offences against children – e.g. sexual assault.
- Class E: Burglary etc. – Domestic and Non-Domestic and 'going equipped to steal'.
- Class F- K: Theft and Fraud etc. – e.g. possession of articles for use in frauds; counterfeiting notes and coins.
- Class H: Miscellaneous lesser offences – e.g. – Possession of Class B or C drug.
- Class I: Offences against public justice and similar offences – e.g. Intimidating Witnesses
- Class J: Serious sexual offences, offences against children – e.g. Trafficking out of UK for sexual exploitation

A quick look at a snapshot of the Crown Prosecution's categories of offences demonstrates how crime is socially

Class H: Miscellaneous lesser offences

Absconding by person released on bail	Bail Act 1976 s6(1), (2)	H
Agreeing to indemnify sureties	Bail Act 1976 s9(1)	H
Being drunk on aircraft	Civil Aviation Act 1982 s60 and 61	H
Acts outraging public decency	Common law	H
Keeping an disorderly house	Common law; Disorderly Houses Act 1751 s8	H
Breach of anti-social behaviour order	Crime and Disorder Act 1998 s1(10)	H
Breach of sex offender order	Crime and Disorder Act 1998 s2(8)	H
Racially-aggravated public order offence	Crime and Disorder Act 1998 s31(1)	H
Racially-aggravated harassment/putting another in fear of violence	Crime and Disorder Act 1998 s32(1)	H
Having an article with a blade or point in a public place	Criminal Justice Act 1988 s139	H

constructed – more acts become criminal as the law evolves. The table on page 2 shows how a whole raft of behaviours suddenly became 'constructed' as criminal following the 1998 criminal justice act, such as breaching an ASBO (ASBOs didn't exist prior to 1998!).

The Criminal Justice System (FYI)

For those that are charged, they will either appear in Magistrates' Court or the Crown Court.

Magistrates' Courts

Virtually all criminal cases start in the Magistrates' courts. The less serious offences are handled entirely in the magistrates' court. Over 95% of all cases are dealt with in this way. The more serious offences are passed on to the Crown Court, to be dealt with by a judge and jury.

Magistrates mainly deal with

- Summary offences. These are less serious cases, such as motoring offences and minor assaults, where the defendant is not entitled to trial by jury and

- Either-way offences. As the name implies, these can be dealt with either by the magistrates or before a judge and jury at the Crown Court. Such offences include theft and handling stolen goods. A suspect can insist on their right to trial in the Crown Court. Similarly, magistrates can decide that a case is sufficiently serious that it should be dealt with in the Crown Court – which can impose tougher punishments.

If a case is to be dealt with in the Magistrates' Court, the defendant will have to enter a plea. If they plead guilty or if they are later found to be guilty, the magistrates can impose a sentence of up to six months imprisonment or a fine of up to £5,000. If the defendant is found not guilty (if they are 'acquitted'), they are judged innocent in the eyes of the law and should be free to go – provided there are no other cases against them outstanding.

Crown Court

Because of the seriousness of offences tried in the Crown Court, these trials take place with a judge and jury. The Crown Court deals with Indictable-only offences such as murder, manslaughter, rape and robbery or less serious offences that are too complex for the magistrate's court

If the defendant is found not guilty, they are discharged and no conviction is recorded against their name. If the defendant is found guilty, they are sentenced and the courts can impose four levels of sentence, depending on the seriousness of the offence:

- Discharges

- Fines

- Community sentences

- Imprisonment

When deciding what sentence to impose, magistrates and judges have to take account of both the facts of the case and the circumstances of the offender.

A sentence needs to:

- Protect the public;

- Punish the offender fairly and appropriately;

- Encourage the offender to make amends for their crime;

- Contribute to crime reduction by stopping re-offending.

26 October 2020

What are the most common types of crime in England & Wales?

The latest figures from the Crime Survey for England and Wales (CSEW) for the year ending June 2023 showed that total crime decreased by 10% (to an estimated 8.4 million offences) compared with the year ending June 2022, mainly caused by decreases in fraud and criminal damage offences. This follows the long-term downward trend and recent falls since the beginning of the coronavirus (COVID-19) pandemic, with total crime 18% lower than the year ending March 2020. Compared with the previous year, estimates for individual crime types showed that:

- criminal damage decreased by 28%

- fraud decreased by 13%

- and computer misuse increased by 33%

Did you know that the UK is no stranger to crime? As teenagers, it's essential to be aware of the most prevalent types of criminal activities in our country. In this article, we will explore the various forms of crime that occur in the UK. By understanding these crimes, you can better protect yourself and your communities.

Unfortunately, crime remains a problem in the UK. According to recent statistics, there were over 5 million recorded criminal offences in 2019 alone, ranging from theft to violent crimes. These numbers may sound alarming, but by learning about the most common types of crime, you can be better prepared to prevent them.

Types of Crime in the UK:

Theft

One of the most common types of crime is theft. This occurs when someone unlawfully takes your belongings without permission. Pickpocketing, shoplifting, and stealing from homes or cars are some examples. Locking doors, being cautious in crowded places, and keeping valuables secure can help prevent theft.

Burglary

Burglary is when someone breaks into a property to steal valuables. It often happens when homes are unoccupied, during holidays or when owners are away. Installing security systems, using timers for lights, and letting trusted neighbours know about your absence are great preventive measures.

Crime estimates from the Crime Survey for England and Wales (CSEW)
December 1981 to June 2023

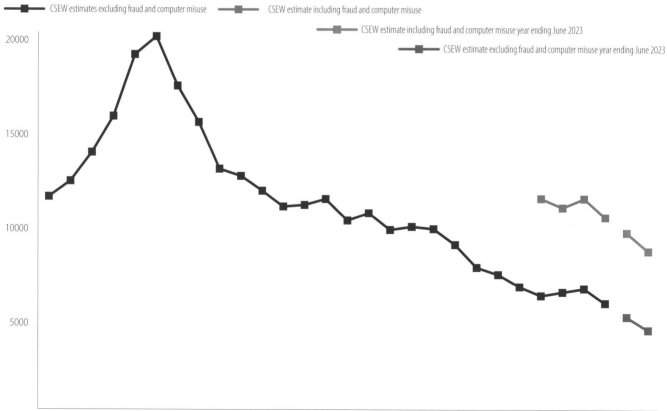

Source: Crime Survey for England and Wales (CSEW) from the Office for National Statistics

Drug Offences

Drug offences involve the possession, distribution, or manufacturing of illegal substances. Drugs can have dangerous consequences, leading to addiction, health problems, and involvement in other criminal activities. Avoid peer pressure and make wise choices to steer clear of drug-related offences.

Violent Crimes

Violent crimes include assault, robbery, and even murder. They involve causing harm or the threat of harm to others. Alcohol-related violence can be a particular issue, especially in city centres and during weekends. Preventing violence and assault necessitates promoting education and awareness about violence prevention, fostering conflict resolution skills, and encouraging community involvement and support.

Cybercrime

In this digital age, cybercrime has become increasingly prevalent. It covers a range of offences, including hacking, online fraud, identity theft, and cyberstalking. Criminals exploit vulnerabilities in computer systems and networks to conduct illicit activities. To protect against cybercrime, individuals should practise strong password management, regularly update their devices and software, exercise caution when sharing personal information online, and use reputable security software.

Anti-Social Behaviour

Anti-social behaviour encompasses a wide range of activities that cause harassment, alarm, and distress to others. This can include nuisance behaviour, noise disturbances, public drunkenness, and graffiti. Addressing anti-social behaviour requires community involvement, encouragement of responsible citizenship, and the creation of safe public spaces. Local authorities and law enforcement agencies play a vital role in enforcing regulations to combat this type of crime.

Domestic Violence

Domestic violence is a serious crime that can have devastating consequences for individuals and families. It encompasses physical, sexual, psychological, or financial abuse within intimate relationships. Addressing domestic violence requires a robust framework that includes early intervention and support programs for victims, education on healthy relationships, and improved access to legal protection and counselling services.

Hate Crimes

Hate crimes are offences motivated by prejudice or hostility towards a person's race, religion, sexual orientation, disability, or other characteristics. These crimes not only harm individuals but also perpetuate social divisions and undermine community cohesion. Combating hate crimes involves raising awareness, promoting tolerance and understanding, and supporting victims while ensuring those responsible are brought to justice.

Prevention and Reporting:

Protect Yourself

To protect yourself, always be aware of your surroundings, especially in unfamiliar areas. Walk with confidence and trust your instincts; if something feels wrong, it probably is. Stay in well-lit areas at night, avoid isolated places, and try to walk with friends whenever possible.

Reporting a Crime

If you witness or are a victim of a crime, it's essential to report it promptly. Call emergency services, such as the police, on 999 in emergencies. For non-emergencies, you can dial 101 to reach your local police. Sharing information and cooperating with the police can help catch criminals and prevent future crimes.

Crime is an unfortunate reality, but it is important to note that these are just some of the most common types of crime in the UK, and there are many other categories and subcategories as well.

By understanding the most prevalent types of crime in the UK, we can play an active role in deterring criminal activities. Stay vigilant, inform others, and be a proactive citizen within your community. Remember, knowledge is power, so let's work together to create safer environments for everyone.

Stay informed, stay safe.

Types of crime

Major class	Definition	Minor classes
Burglary	Burglary is the theft, or attempted theft from a premises where access is not authorised. Any damaged caused in the attempt to access that premises is also counted as burglary.	Burglary in a dwelling Burglary in other buildings
Criminal Damage	Where property is intentionally destroyed or damaged.	Criminal damage to dwelling Criminal damage to motor vehicle Criminal damage to other building Other criminal damage
Drugs	Possession, consumption, supply of or the intent to supply illegal drugs.	Drug trafficking Other drugs Possession of drugs
Fraud & Forgery	Fraud is an intentional deception, usually for monetary gain. Forgery is the action of creating a replica of an object with the intention of deception.	Other fraud and forgery
Robbery	Theft with the use of force or a threat of force.	Business property Personal property
Sexual Offences	Sexual offences include; Indecent Assault, sexual offences against children, non consentual offences, sexual exploitation.	Other sexual Rape
Theft & Handling	Theft is 'dishonestly appropriates property belonging to another with the intention of permanently depriving the other of it'. Handling is receiving goods or assisting in the retention, removal, disposal or realization for another, knowing or believing them to be stolen.	Handling stolen goods Motor vehicle interference and tampering Other theft Theft from motor vehicle Theft from shops Theft person Theft/taking of motor vehicle Theft/taking of pedal cycle
Violence Against The Person	Violence Against The Person refers to a broad array of criminal offences which usually involve bodily harm, the threat of bodily harm, or other actions committed against the will of an individual. Can also include crimes that do not include bodily harm such as harassment and stalking.	Assault with injury Common assault Harassment Murder (homicide) Offensive weapon Other violence Wounding/GBH

There are many types of crime that are not listed here such as driving and traffic offences, anti-social behaviour, cybercrime etc.

There are also some crimes in the UK that you may not be aware of such as:

- Flying a kite in public
- Being drunk on the street, in a pub or in a restaurant
- Vacuuming between the hours of 6pm & 8am on a weekday or 1pm & 8am on a Saturday or on a Sunday
- Defacing a banknote or destroying a coin
- No walking cows down the street in daylight
- Dressing up as a police officer or in military gear
- Using a phone to pay at a drive-through

Are crime rates at a record high?

By Tony Thompson

What was claimed	**Our verdict**
Crime rates in England and Wales are at a record high.	This claim is missing context. While the number of crimes recorded by the police has risen, this is not the best data to understand overall trends. Overall crime as measured by the Crime Survey for England and Wales is actually falling.

'Crime in England and Wales hits record high' – *Daily Mirror*, 27 October 2022.

An article in the *Daily Mirror* claims that crime rates in England and Wales are at a record high.

The article says: 'Some 6.5 million offences have been logged in the past year, up 12% on the previous 12 months. The rise has been fuelled by an increase in sex crimes, up 20%, and violent attacks, up 13%, says the Office for National Statistics [ONS].'

Sky News had also covered the figures with a tweet headlined: 'Crime in England and Wales hits all-time high'. This tweet has since been deleted.

While it is true that the latest ONS figures show that the number of crimes recorded by police has risen significantly, the figures do not tell the whole story, as not all crimes are reported, so quoting these statistics in isolation can give a misleading impression of the levels of offending.

While the number of police recorded crimes is currently at a record high, survey data suggests that overall crime fell by 8% between the year to March 2020 and the year to June 2022.

So is crime up or down?

In addition to police recorded crime statistics, the ONS publishes data from the Crime Survey for England and Wales (CSEW) which estimates the level of offending by conducting interviews with a sample of 13,500 people and extrapolating the results across the entire population.

While police recorded crime figures reflect the number of people who have made formal reports of offences, the researchers conducting the CSEW ask people if they have been a victim of a crime. The results are recorded regardless of whether that crime was reported to the police.

According to research agency Kantar Public, which conducts the survey on behalf of the ONS, only 4 in 10 crimes are reported to the police. This explains why the number of crimes reported by the CSEW is higher than the number of offences recorded by police.

The ONS says: 'The CSEW is a better indicator of long-term trends for the crime types and population it covers, than police recorded crime because it is unaffected by changes in levels of reporting to the police or police recording practices.'

Because both the nature of crime and the collection of crime statistics was so disrupted by the pandemic, the ONS compares the latest data for the year to June 2022 against the year to March 2020, the last undisrupted by the pandemic.

Over this time period, the overall level of crime fell 8%. The ONS in particular noted a fall in the prevalence of theft during the pandemic has been sustained, and that an increase in fraud and computer misuse crimes during the pandemic has fallen back to pre-pandemic, and below pre-pandemic levels respectively.

Police numbers

Police recorded crime figures are not so reliable in understanding the total level of crime, but are extremely reliable for high-harm crimes such as murder, which are almost always reported.

In many instances, the prevalence of such crimes have fallen. For example, the police recorded 679 homicide offences in the year ending June 2022, a 5% decrease compared with the year ending March 2020 though an increase of 13% compared to the year ending June 2021 when some lockdown restrictions were still in place.

Although the story in the *Mirror* noted that homicides and knife crime were below pre-pandemic levels, it did not mention that it was referring to police recorded crime figures or that the CSEW said overall crime was falling.

The latest figures also show falls in burglary, robbery and firearms-enabled crime, among others, compared to just before the pandemic.

With respect to domestic abuse and sexual offences, the ONS said that the number of police recorded incidents had increased compared to pre-pandemic levels, but there was no significant change in the prevalence as measured by the Crime Survey.

The ONS says: 'The Crime Survey for England and Wales (CSEW) provides a more reliable measure of long-term trends in domestic abuse, sexual assault, stalking, and harassment than police recorded crime data.'

It warns that while police recorded crime may pick up on genuine changes in crime levels, some increases are also influenced by changes in the way crimes are recorded, the introduction of new offences and more victims reporting crime.

28 October 2022

Recorded crime in Scotland at one of the lowest levels seen since 1974

By Andrew Learmonth

The number of rapes and attempted rapes in Scotland has hit a record high, according to the latest recorded crime figures.

They showed a 5% increase on last year, up from 2,455 to 2,567 crimes. They were also up by 4% from the year ending June 2019.

Glasgow recorded more rapes and attempted rapes than anywhere else in Scotland, though the 326 reported in the city was down 4% on the previous year.

Edinburgh saw a 7% increase, up from 218 to 234.

Dundee jumped from 102 to 126, an increase of 24%, while Aberdeen recorded 99, a fall of 7%.

The largest percentage increase was in Orkney, where numbers jumped from 8 in the year ending June 2022 to 16 last year.

In total, there were 14,834 sexual crimes recorded, down from 14,880 in the previous year.

While there were falls in the number of sexual assaults and crimes associated with prostitution, there was a significant increase in the number of crimes involving indecent photos of children, up from 683 to 795 crimes, a jump of 16%. That's an increase of 50% from the year ending June 2019.

Sandy Brindley, the Chief Executive of Rape Crisis, said she was concerned by the 'very high numbers of sexual crimes' being reported.

'These figures aren't just numbers. They represent the experience of survivors who have made the often very difficult decision to report.

'But it's important to remember that the majority of survivors of rape and sexual violence never report the incident and their experiences are not reflected in these statistics.

'If and when a survivor is ready to report support throughout the entire process is available from local Rape Crisis centres across Scotland.'

Number of recorded crimes/offences
(Thousands)

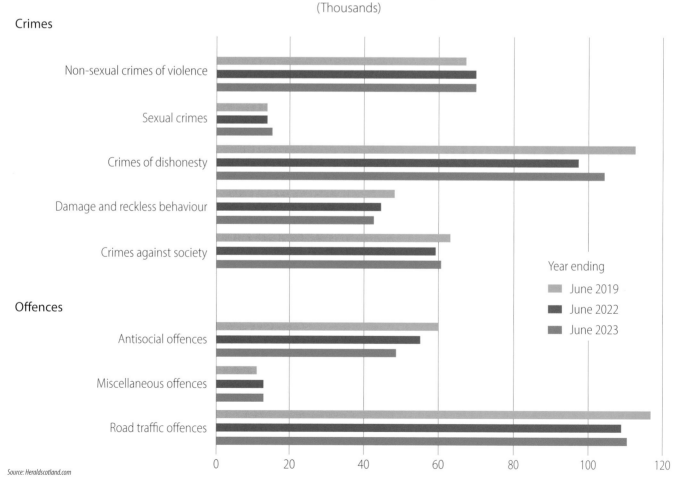

Source: Heraldscotland.com

The statistics also showed an increase in murder and culpable homicide, up by 8% compared to the previous year, from 50 to 54 crimes, though this is a significant decrease from the year ending June 2019 when 74 crimes were recorded.

There was also a drop in the number of serious assaults and attempted murders, down by 8% on the last year, and 22% from 2019.

Overall, police in Scotland recorded 292,702 crimes in the year ending June 2023, up by 2% on the previous year, but 4% lower than the 305,300 crimes recorded in the year ending June 2019.

Cabinet Secretary for Justice and Home Affairs Angela Constance said the statistics showed that Scotland 'continues to be a safe place to live.'

She added: 'These continued low levels of crime are due to the efforts across policing, justice and community safety partners to deliver safer communities and our investment in the justice system.

'With recorded crime remaining at one of the lowest levels seen since 1974, the latest figures show reductions in crimes such as violence, sexual crimes and damage and reckless behaviour.

'We will continue to focus on crime prevention, reducing reoffending and supporting victims of crime.

'That is why we are investing £1.45 billion in policing in 2023-24, increasing the resource budget by 6.3%, an additional £80 million, despite difficult financial circumstances due to UK Government austerity and our fixed budget.'

Non-sexual crimes of violence were less than 1% lower compared to the previous year, while crimes of dishonesty were 7% higher.

Death by dangerous driving increased by 18% compared to the previous year, up from 39 to 46 crimes and increased by 7% from the year ending June 2019.

Shoplifting increased by 21% compared to the previous year (from 24,877 to 30,202 crimes), but decreased by 10% from the year ending June 2019 (from 33,611 to 30,202 crimes).

Fraud increased by 3% compared to the previous year (from 16,461 to 16,956 crimes), and increased by 82% from the year ending June 2019 (from 9,310 to 16,956 crimes). Further explanation on the changes in levels of recorded fraud are available in the Recorded Crime in Scotland annual bulletin.

Urinating etc. decreased by 41% compared to last year, down from 1,590 to 932 offences. Down by 63% from the year ending June 2019, when 2,490 offences were recorded.

The Scottish Conservative shadow justice secretary Russell Findlay called the rise in the number of rapes 'deeply alarming.'

He criticised new sentencing guidelines introduced in January last year, which make rehabilitation rather than punishment a primary consideration for under 25s.

At the time, the Scottish Sentencing Council said the new rules were based on 'compelling scientific evidence on the development of cognitive maturity.'

However, they came under scrutiny in April when Sean Hogg was given a community sentence for raping a 13-year-old girl.

Mr Findlay said: 'The under-25 sentencing guidelines as well as use of diversion from prosecution means that some rapists are not being held to account.

'Shop staff and retailers say they're under siege from shoplifters who think they can steal with impunity because they're only likely to get a slap on the wrists.

'This crimewave comes against a backdrop of the SNP presiding over the lowest officer numbers since 2008 and allowing certain crimes in the North East to no longer even be investigated.

'The justice secretary needs to properly fund our police and our hardworking officers otherwise our communities will be put at even greater risk.'

Scottish Labour Justice spokesperson Pauline McNeill said: 'Alarm bells should be ringing' over the figures.

'But to anyone who has been following the SNP's chaotic approach to policing they come as no surprise.

'For years the SNP has allowed our police force to become under-resourced, understaffed, and overworked – and it is our communities who pay the price.

'This is the worst police budget since devolution. Victims of crime are being let down by a government that sticks its head in the sand and has left Scotland's criminal justice system in tatters.

'The SNP must get serious about tackling crime. They can start by investing in our police force and ensuring criminals once again actually face the letter of the law.'

19 September 2023

Key Facts

- Police in Scotland recorded 292,702 crimes in the year ending June 2023, up by 2% on the previous year, but 4% lower than the 305,300 crimes recorded in the year ending June 2019.

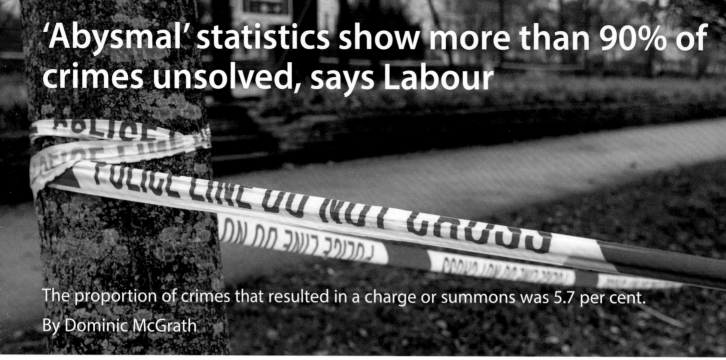

'Abysmal' statistics show more than 90% of crimes unsolved, says Labour

The proportion of crimes that resulted in a charge or summons was 5.7 per cent.

By Dominic McGrath

Only 5.7 per cent of crimes were solved by police last year, according to new figures, as Labour condemned the government's 'abysmal' record on law and order.

Home Office data for England and Wales, released earlier this month, revealed the proportion of crimes that resulted in a charge or summons was 5.7 per cent, although that figure represented a small increase on the previous year.

The data, which covers a 12-month period from April 2022 onwards, showed that 2.3 million crimes were dropped without a suspect being found.

The charge rate for sexual offences was 3.6 per cent, with rape at 2.1 per cent.

Only 6.5 per cent of robbery offences ended with someone being charged.

Shadow home secretary Yvette Cooper said the figures were a 'national scandal' as Labour pledged to boost the numbers of crimes solved if the party wins the next election.

The opposition said it would introduce a new requirement for police forces to run direct recruitment of detectives to reverse a national shortage, with plans to bring in individuals from fields such as business fraud investigations and child protection.

Labour said fewer than half of police forces have such a scheme currently.

Ms Cooper said: 'After 13 years of Tory government, over 90 per cent of crimes are going unsolved.

'That is the abysmal Conservative record on law and order – more criminals being let off and more victims being let down.

'For some serious crimes, like rape and robbery, the charge rate is now so low it constitutes a national scandal.

'For far too long in this country, too many crimes have been committed without any consequences. Victims increasingly feel like no-one comes and nothing is done. Labour is determined this has to change.'

A Home Office spokesperson said: 'Since 2010, our communities are safer – with neighbourhood crimes including burglary, robbery and theft down 51 per cent and serious violent crime down 46 per cent.

'The government has delivered more police officers than ever in England and Wales and the Home Secretary expects police to improve public confidence by getting the basics right – catching more criminals and delivering justice for victims.

'As part of the Beating Crime Plan, we have also committed to giving every single person in England and Wales access to the police digitally through a national online platform.

'This will allow the public to access a range of interactive police services in one place, including information on neighbourhood police officers and their contact details, allowing them to raise concerns with neighbourhood officers directly.'

Policing minister Chris Philp accused Labour of being 'soft on crime and soft on criminals'.

He said: 'Where Labour are in power, crime is over a third higher than Conservative-run areas, and Sir Keir Starmer whipped his MPs to vote against tougher sentences for rapists and murderers, as well as campaigning to keep dangerous foreign criminals in the UK.

'Under the Conservatives, adult rape convictions have increased by two-thirds over the last year, dangerous criminals are being locked up for longer, and there are now over 20,000 new police officers helping to keep our streets safe.'

31 July 2023

Being charged with a crime

If you're charged with a crime you'll be given a 'charge sheet'. This sets out the details of the crime you're being charged with.

The police will decide if you:

- can be released from police custody until the court hearing - but you might have to follow certain rules, known as 'bail'
- are kept in police custody until you're taken to court for your hearing

Your first court hearing after you're charged with a crime will be at a magistrates' court - even if your trial will be at a Crown Court later on.

If you're charged with a minor offence your case could be decided without going to court ('single justice procedure'). If you get a single justice procedure notice you must respond within 21 days.

There are different rules if you're charged with a crime in Scotland or charged with a crime in Northern Ireland.

Young people

If you're under 18, your first hearing will usually be at a youth court.

If you're under 17, the police must arrange for you to be held in local authority accommodation, if possible, before you go to court.

If you're aged 12 to 16, the police can decide to keep you at the police station if they think it will protect the public.

Bail

When you're waiting for a court hearing or a trial, you might be given bail. This means you can be released from custody until the hearing or the trial.

Bail from a police station

You can be given bail at the police station after you've been charged. This means you'll be released from custody until your first court hearing.

If you're given bail, you might have to agree to conditions like:

- living at a particular address
- not contacting certain people
- giving your passport to the police so you cannot leave the UK
- reporting to a police station at agreed times, for example once a week

If you do not stick to these conditions you can be arrested again and be taken to prison to wait for your court hearing.

Bail from a court

When you've been charged and you attend your hearing at a magistrates' court, you might be given bail until your trial begins.

You may not be given bail if:

- you've been convicted of a crime in the past
- you've been given bail in the past and not stuck to the terms
- the court thinks you might not turn up for your next hearing
- the court thinks you might commit a crime while you're on bail

If you're given bail, you might have to agree to conditions like:

- living at a particular address
- not contacting certain people
- giving up your passport so you cannot leave the UK

If you do not stick to these conditions, you can be arrested again. You'll stay in police custody until you're given another court hearing.

The court may put different conditions in place for your bail or keep you in prison until your trial starts.

Remand

If the court decides to put you on remand it means you'll go to prison until your trial begins.

If you're under 18 you'll be taken to a secure centre for young people, not an adult prison.

You may be put on remand if:

- you've been convicted of a crime in the past
- the court thinks you might not go to your court hearing
- the court thinks you might commit a crime while on bail
- you have been given bail before and not stuck to the terms

If you are arrested

What happens when you arrive at the police station?

When you arrive at the police station you should be told what your rights are (these will be written on a piece of paper but if you don't understand what it means you should ask questions).

You have the right to:

* Have someone told that you have been arrested (for example, you might ask a police officer to call your parent/s or guardian/s

* Have a solicitor and talk to them on your own/in private.

* Have medical help if you are feeling ill

* See the rules the police must follow (Code of Practice)

* If you are under 17 years old, you also have the right to have an appropriate adult with you at the police station and to talk to them in private if you want to. If you are under 18 the police must try to contact your parents, guardian or carers.

Can you have someone with you when you are interviewed by the police?

Yes, if you are under 18 years old then the custody officer must find out who is responsible for your welfare. This may be your parent or guardian, or you may have an appropriate adult appointed by a Local Authority or organisation or another adult that you trust.

The appropriate adult can be with you during the interview to comfort and explain legal terms to you, ensure that you understand the questions being asked and that your rights and interests are being protected.

You are also entitled to have a duty solicitor with you when you are being interviewed.

An appropriate adult can be a parent, guardian, carer, social worker, another family member or friend aged 18 or over, or a volunteer aged 18 or over.

Do you have a right to silence?

No, not really. When the police arrest you they will caution you, this is when they say 'You do not have to say anything, but it may harm your defence if you do not mention when questioned something which you later rely on in court…'.

This means that if you remain silent in your interview with the police and then later explain your actions when you are in court, the judge and jury might wonder why you didn't say that to the police from the start. They might then decide not to believe what you have said in court.

How long can the police hold you at the police station for?

There are limits on how long the police can hold you at the police station before they charge you. You can be held for 24 hours if the police think that you have committed an offence. Another 12 hours can be added onto this if the offence they think that you have committed is serious.

Sometimes, but not often, the police will ask the court whether you can be held for longer. The court can only allow the police to hold you for an extra 96 hours (4 days) before you are charged. You can be held for up to 14 days if you are arrested under a Terrorism Act.

When can the police search you at the police station?

The police can search you when you arrive at the police station and at any time while you are held in custody.

If the police think that you might have something hidden on or in your body they can do a strip search. This is an intimate search and you will need to remove more than just your outer clothing. Such a search must be carried out by an officer of the same sex as you, in a place where you cannot be seen by anyone who does not need to be there and no-one of the opposite sex is allowed to be there.

If you are under 17 years old, you should have an adult that you know and trust with you (your parent or guardian for example) although you don't have to have them there if you don't want to. As soon as the search is over you should be allowed to get dressed.

Can the police take photographs, fingerprints or other samples?

If you are 14 years old or younger, your parent(s) or guardian(s) have to agree before the police take your photograph or your fingerprints.

If you are aged 15 or 16 both you and your parent or guardian have to agree before the police can take your photograph or fingerprints.

Convictions

Situation	How long can they keep the Fingerprints and DNA for?
If you are convicted at any age or given a youth caution for any recordable offence	There is no limit
If you are convicted under 18 for a minor offence	If it is your first conviction they can keep it for 5 years plus the length of any prison sentence you get
	If your prison sentence is for 5 years or more there is no limit
	If it is your second conviction there is no limit to how long they can keep your fingerprints and DNA

Non-convictions

Situation	How long can they keep the Fingerprints and DNA for?
If you are charged at any age with recordable offence but not convicted	3 years plus a 2 year extension if a District Judge says so
	If you have a previous conviction which is not excluded from the case then there is no limit to how long they can keep your fingerprints and DNA
If you are arrested at any age with a qualifying offence but not charged	3 years if the Biometrics Commissioner says so, plus a 2 year extension if a District Judge says so
	If you have a previous conviction which is not excluded from the case then there is no limit to how long they can keep your fingerprints and DNA
If you are arrested or charged for a minor offence at any age	Unless you have a previous conviction they cannot keep your fingerprints or DNA

If you are older than 16 the police can take your photograph even if you don't agree. The police can also take your fingerprints even if you don't agree to this if they need this information as part of their investigation.

As part of their investigation, the police might also want to take samples of your hair, nails, saliva and other things that can easily be removed from your body. If you haven't been charged, the police need both you and an adult that you trust to agree before they can take these samples, but there are times when they can take these samples even if you don't agree. If you have been charged, the police can take such samples even if you don't agree.

The police need both you and an adult that you trust to agree that it is OK before they take more intimate samples such as blood and urine. You can't be forced to give a sample like this even if you have been charged.

What happens with your fingerprints and other samples?

Your fingerprints or other samples can be kept by the police (even if you are not charged), please see table above for timescales of keeping your data.

You are entitled to a copy of your own police records.

What happens if you are given a reprimand or a final warning?

The police might decide to give you a reprimand or final warning instead of charging you. A reprimand will be given if this is your first minor offence. Therefore, if you have already been convicted of an offence this is not a possibility. A final warning will be given if it is your first offence but it is a serious offence or if you have received a reprimand before. A final warning will be referred to the Youth Offending Team.

Before the police can give you a reprimand or final warning they must have enough evidence to prove that you committed an offence and you must admit that you committed the offence.

Reprimands and final warnings go on your record and can be used against you if you have more trouble with the police so only accept one if you are guilty of an offence, and after speaking to a lawyer. Any individual cannot receive more than two warnings. If you do receive a reprimand or a final warning it will not mean you have a criminal record, however it will result in a police record.

How can you complain about police treatment?

You can complain about how you were treated by any member of police staff. The best way to start is to complain

to the custody officer before you leave the police station. There are many services that you can contact who will help you to make a claim. For example, you can contact Citizen's Advice and they will explain what your rights are and help you to make a complaint. You can also contact the Independent Police Complaints Commission and make a complaint online.

What can you expect if you complain?

- The person dealing with the complaint will contact you to get the details.

- They should ask you what you want to happen.

- You can expect to be listened to and treated fairly.

- You will be kept updated about the progress of your complaint.

- You must receive an update every 28 days.

- When your complaint is finalised, you will be contacted about the outcome and any action that will be taken as a result.

- If you're not happy with the result, you may be able to request a review.

What are the possible outcomes?

The Police may give you an explanation for what happened.

- The Police may provide you with an apology.

- The officers involved could be given training and development.

- The force may change their policies and procedures.

- The officers involved could face disciplinary action.

What if the police charge you with a crime?

You can be charged if the police have enough evidence against you and will be given a charge sheet. The police then have to decide whether to let you out on bail until the time of your trial (this means that you can go home until you go to court) or whether you will need to be detained until your trial. Usually, where you are allowed to go home you will have to agree to certain conditions. If you do not stick to these conditions you can be arrested again.

Between the age of 12-16 you can be kept at the police station if they think you are a danger to the public. Usually, children and young people are released on bail unless the custody officer has a good reason to believe that you should not be. The police can decide to detain you before trial if they think that you will not show up for court, you might commit more crimes or if it would not be safe for you to go home. If aged 17 you must be held in Local Authority Accommodation before court.

The police will refer you to a Youth Offending Team, and they will work with you before and after your trial to try to work out why you have committed an offence and make sure that you don't do it again.

Age and the Law in the UK: understanding your rights and responsibilities

As you navigate through your teenage years and inch closer to adulthood, it's important to understand the various legal rights and responsibilities that come with different ages in the UK. Knowing your rights is empowering, and being aware of the laws will help you make informed choices. So, let's dive into the world of age and the law!

Starting right from birth, the law is there to protect us. The age of consent for medical treatment without parental consent is actually quite low, at just 16. That means if you need medical attention or advice, you can seek it without your parents' involvement. It's great to know that your health is your priority and that the law is on your side. Moving on to school, education is compulsory for all children between the ages of 5 and 18 in the UK.

When it comes to working part-time, many teenagers start exploring job opportunities to gain some independence and pocket money. However, the legal age to work varies in different types of jobs. For most types of work, including part-time jobs, you need to be at least 14 years old. But, if you're eager to work in paid entertainment, such as television or theatre, you'll have to wait until you're at least 16.

Alright, let's address the topic that probably intrigues many of you – the age of consent. In the UK, the legal age of consent for sexual activity is 16. It's important to note that this applies to heterosexual and homosexual relationships. However, it's crucial to remember that consent should always be given freely and willingly by all parties involved. Your emotional well-being and safety should never be compromised, so make sure you are ready and comfortable before taking any steps in that direction.

Now, let's talk about driving – every teenager's dream. The legal driving age in the UK is 17 if you want to drive a car, and 16 if you want to ride a moped or light quad bike. It's exciting to look forward to that independence of being able to explore new places on your own terms. Just remember to always follow the rules of the road and drive safely! As you reach 18, congratulations, you've officially become an adult in the UK! You can now vote, drink alcohol in a pub, and even get married. Reaching this milestone means embracing a whole new set of responsibilities, like paying taxes and making decisions that shape your future. It's an exciting time but remember to tread responsibly and make choices that are right for you.

Remember, this article provides only a brief overview of the age and the law in the UK. Laws can be complex, so make sure to seek legal advice or consult official resources if you have specific questions or concerns. Understanding your rights and responsibilities is vital for making responsible decisions and enjoying your teenage years to the fullest.

Birth

From the day we are born, there are certain legal protections that we are entitled to. For example, the law requires that we are registered with the government within 42 days of birth. Additionally, there are strict laws surrounding child protection and welfare, ensuring that every child is entitled to a safe and nurturing environment.

Age 4

At the age of 4, children in the UK typically start primary school. This marks the beginning of their formal education and a new phase in their lives. From this age, children also have to follow specific rules in public places, such as not causing harm or damaging property.

Age 10

At age 10, children in the UK become criminally responsible for their actions. This means that if a child commits a serious crime, such as theft or assault, they can be prosecuted in a court of law. It is crucial for teenagers to understand the consequences of their actions and make responsible choices.

Age 12

At age 12, children in the UK can be taken to a magistrates' court if they commit a less serious crime. This may involve being given a reprimand or a final warning.

These measures are designed to prevent children from committing further crimes and help them get back on the right track.

Age 14

From the age of 14, teenagers in the UK can get a part-time job and earn their own money. However, there are limitations on the types of work and the number of hours they can work. It is essential to know the laws around child employment to ensure a safe and fair working environment.

Age 16

At age 16, teenagers in the UK become eligible for several new legal rights and responsibilities. These include:

- Leaving school and legally working full-time, with certain restrictions.
- Obtaining some benefits and financial assistance independently.
- Joining or changing political parties, expressing their political opinions and participating in democratic processes.
- Getting married or entering into a civil partnership if you live in Scotland or Northern Ireland.
- Applying for a passport without parental consent.

Age 17

When teenagers reach the age of 17, they become eligible to:

- Drive a car or motorcycle after passing their driving test (with appropriate licence and insurance).
- Donate blood and potentially save lives.

Age 18

The age of 18 is a significant milestone in the UK as it marks the transition into adulthood. At this age, individuals are legally allowed to:

- Watch films with a rating of 18 in cinemas, as their own choice of entertainment widens.
- Vote in all elections, enabling them to have a say in the democratic process.
- Buy alcohol and consume it responsibly in pubs or restaurants.
- Purchase and use tobacco products.
- Apply for a credit card and manage their own finances.
- Enter into a contract, including signing a tenancy agreement or taking out a loan.
- Get a tattoo or piercing without parental consent.
- Get married or enter into a civil partnership in England and Wales.

10 reasons why ten is too young

At 10 years of age, we have one of the lowest ages of criminal responsibility in the world and the lowest in Europe. Despite repeated calls from the international children's rights community and a large number of organisations working with children and young people here in Northern Ireland to raise the age, no progress has been made.

On 3rd October 2022 the Department of Justice issued a 12 week public consultation on increasing the minimum age of criminal responsibility in Northern Ireland from 10 years to 14 years.

In compliance with international children's rights standards NIACRO, VOYPIC, Include Youth and the Children's Law Centre are calling for the minimum age of criminal responsibility to be raised to 16 years, with no exceptions for serious or grave offences.

10 reasons

REASON 1: It does not comply with international children's rights standards

The United Nations Committee on the Rights of the Child has repeatedly said that the minimum age of criminal responsibility in the UK is not compatible with the government's obligations under international standards of juvenile justice and the United Nations Convention on the Rights of the Child (UNCRC).

A recent report submitted in December 2020 to the UN Committee on the Rights of the Child in preparation for the next examination of the UK Government's compliance with the UNCRC, compiled by the Children's Law Centre and drawing on evidence submitted by a range of organisations in NI stated:

'Despite a "Raise the Age" campaign involving organisations working with children and young people, the Northern Ireland Commissioner for Children and Young People, and children's rights advocates, the age of criminal responsibility in Northern Ireland remains 10 years. This contravenes international standards, including the Global Study on Children Deprived of Liberty which argued that states should establish a MACR "which shall not be below 14 years of age".'

The UN Committee on the Rights of the Child recommend that the minimum age of criminal responsibility should be 16 years. This position is based on extensive global evidence on the harm having a low age of criminal responsibility has, the ineffectiveness of such an approach and on the improved understanding of child and adolescent development.

'States parties are encouraged to take note of recent scientific findings, and to increase their minimum age accordingly, to at least 14 years of age. Moreover, the developmental and neuroscience evidence indicates that adolescent brains continue to mature even beyond the teenage years, affecting certain kinds of decision-making.

'Therefore, the Committee commends States parties that have a higher minimum age, for instance 15 or 16 years of age.' (UNCRC, 2019, General Comment No.24 on children's rights in the justice system)

When delivering the Children's Law Centre 2008 Annual Lecture, the then Chair of the Committee stated:

'The Committee clearly stated the importance of raising it to 12 with a view of eventually raising it even further... In order to persuade State parties to seriously raising the age of criminal responsibility... 12 was decided as the absolute minimum age by the Committee... Furthermore, it was the general understanding of the Committee that industrialised, democratic societies would go even further as to raising it to even a higher age, such as 14 or 16'

We have an opportunity to go beyond the bare minimum of what a children's rights compliant age of criminal responsibility should be. Our health and social care agencies and our voluntary and community sector are mature and developed meaning that we are able to provide an alternative pathway for children, that does not necessitate branding them as a criminal from a young age. We should not aspire to just meet the lowest age threshold of what is acceptable in terms of the age of criminal responsibility. Rather we should aim for a position which sets us out as exemplary in terms of how we treat our vulnerable children. When the UN Committee on the Rights of the Child 'commends' State parties that have a higher minimum age such as 16 we should be aiming to reach a point of commendation rather than just the 'at least' option.

REASON 2: Experts tell us 10 is too low

Following the devolution of justice to the Northern Ireland Assembly, the Minister of Justice launched an independent review of the youth justice system in Northern Ireland which was to take into account international human rights standards, including the United Nations Convention on the Rights of the Child (UNCRC). The independent team of experts with a wide experience in the field of youth justice and law carried out an extensive review of the youth justice system in Northern Ireland. They were supported by a Reference Group made up of renowned academics and senior decision makers. Following a lengthy analysis of reports, inspections, policy papers, written submissions and engagement with many individuals and groups, including children and young people, they presented a series of recommendations.

One of these was that the age of criminal responsibility should be raised to 12 with immediate effect and that following a period of no more than three years, consideration should be given to raise it to 14. David Ford, Minister of Justice at that time, confirmed that the public consultation on the review showed substantial support for the age to be raised and publicly stated that he personally favours an increase to 12 or 14. Subsequent Ministers of Justice have also supported an increase in the age of criminal responsibility. The UN Committee on the Rights of the Child recommend that the minimum age of criminal responsibility should be 16 years.

The recommendation relating to the minimum age of criminal responsibility from the independent review team was made in 2011.

Ten years later, no progress has been made.

REASON 3: Our age of criminal responsibility is at the bottom of the league

We have one of the lowest ages of criminal responsibility in the world and one of the lowest in Europe. The worldwide trend is to raise the age, generally to at least 14.

The table below outlines the minimum age of criminal responsibility across European countries.

England and Wales also have a minimum age of criminal responsibility of 10 years. In the Republic of Ireland, the age has been raised to 12 for all but the most serious offences. In Scotland, the Scottish Law Commission recommended that the age should be raised to 12.

The Age of Criminal Responsibility (Scotland) Act 2019 was passed unanimously by the Scottish Parliament on 7th May 2019, received Royal Assent on 11th June 2019 and fully commenced on 17th December 2021. This Act raised the age of criminal responsibility in Scotland from 8 to 12. Additionally, it provides certain safeguards to ensure that harmful behaviour by children under 12 can be responded to in an appropriate and meaningful way, which will not criminalise children.

There have been calls in Scotland to go beyond raising the age to 12, with considerable support from key stakeholders to raise the age to 16. The Children's Commissioner for Scotland has called for the minimum age of criminal responsibility to be raised to 16 years old claiming that an increase to only 12 years of age is a significant missed opportunity. There have also been calls for an increase in the age in England and Wales from some Parliamentarians, academics, NGOs and civil society. Lord Dholakia has repeatedly introduced bills into the House of Lords aimed at raising the age. Lord Thomas of Cwmgiedd, the former Lord Chief Justice of England and Wales, has also called for an increase stating:

'There are better ways to deal with children than criminalising them. The current age of criminal responsibility is too young. It does not comply with the United Nations Convention on the Rights of the Child.'

The minimum age of criminal responsibility across European countries

Albania	14	Luxembourg	18
Andorra	12	Macedonia	14
Armenia	16	Malta	14
Austria	14	Moldova	16
Azerbaijan	16	Monaco	13
Belarus	16	Montenegro	14
Belgium	18	Netherlands	12
Bosnia & Herzegovina	14	Northern Ireland	10
Bulgaria	14	Norway	15
Croatia	14	Poland	15
Cyprus	14	Portugal	16
Czech Republic	15	Romania	14
Denmark	15	Russian Federation	14
England	10	San Marino	12
Estonia	14	Scotland	12
Finland	15	Serbia	14
France	13	Slovakia	14
Georgia	14	Slovenia	14
Germany	14	Spain	14
Greece	15	Sweden	15
Hungary	14	Switzerland	10
Iceland	15	Turkey	12
Ireland	12	Ukraine	16
Italy	14	Wales	10
Latvia	14		
Liechtenstein	14		
Lithuania	14		

Source: 10 Reasons Why Ten is Too Young, Include Youth

REASON 4: Children at risk of coming into contact with the justice system have complex needs

Children in areas of high deprivation are more likely to be at risk of coming into contact with the criminal justice system and in NI this is particularly true of communities affected by the conflict. The 2011 Youth Justice Review made specific reference to a number of groups of young people that are over-represented in the youth justice system. These included young people with speech and language difficulties, mental health problems and care experienced children.

There is no shortage of research linking the higher risks of young people living with poverty, mental ill health, having experience of being in care or experiencing neglect/abuse, misusing drugs or alcohol, and having learning and behavioural difficulties, coming into contact with the criminal justice system. It is often children who are in greatest social need that are swept up by youth justice systems. Children in care are particularly over-represented in figures of children in custody in Northern Ireland. Of the children in custody during 2021/2022, 34% were in care. In recent DoJ funded research on over-representation in the youth justice system in NI, the authors drew attention to the multiple disadvantages and vulnerabilities that the majority of children who come into contact with the justice system have. These included economic disadvantage, under-resourced communities, conflict legacy, parenting stress, educational disadvantage, and family involvement in the criminal justice system. A low age of criminal responsibility that seeks a criminal justice solution to welfare issues, poverty and adverse childhood experiences, simply accelerates already vulnerable children further into the system and ultimately custody.

REASON 5: The age of criminal responsibility is out of line with other age-related legislation

The age of criminal responsibility is out of step with other legal age limits. Below the age of 18 children cannot vote; sit on a jury; buy alcohol, tobacco or fireworks; get a tattoo or open their own bank account. Below the age of 16 children cannot consent to sex, leave school, play the lottery or buy a pet. How we treat children within the criminal justice system is starkly different to how we treat them in other areas of social policy. There is an inherent unfairness to the standards of accountability we hold children to in this way.

REASON 6: Children's brains are still developing

To apply the same standards of criminal responsibility to a 10 year old as we would to an adult is to ignore large amounts of evidence about the immaturity of children at that age. Children do not have the emotional maturity to be responsible by law for their actions.

Although it is true at 10 children are likely to know the difference between right and wrong, they do not have the capacity to fully understand the consequences of their actions. Neuroscience data has found that there are developmental differences in the brain's biochemistry and anatomy that may limit adolescents' ability to perceive risks, control impulses, understand consequences and control emotions. There is an argument that children are not capable of fully understanding the implications of their behaviour or know how to regulate their behaviour. Evidence on children's understanding of the criminal justice process suggests that 13 years old and younger are impaired in their ability to understand criminal proceedings and only begin to understand what it means to appear before a judge at around 14 or 15 years of age. Evidence also suggests that children who have experienced trauma, abuse or neglect are 'particularly poorly developed in the required capacities for criminal responsibility and are much more likely to come into conflict with the law'. Emerging neuroscience evidence should be one factor to be considered when debating the need to raise the minimum age of criminal responsibility.

Key voices with expertise in child development and child psychiatry are calling for an increase. As Dr Phil Anderson, Consultant Psychiatrist in Child and Adolescent Mental Health, states in his contribution to our blog series on MACR, hosted on the Queen's University Policy Engagement Site, the UNCRC requires that domestic laws are developed in a manner consistent with the emerging capacities of the child. He goes on to say:

'The relevance of these brain findings to youth justice is that the adolescent population is demonstrably and substantially different to the adult population. Legislative approaches to issues, such as MACR, needs to reflect the current scientific understanding of the brain.'

In giving evidence to MPs on the Justice Committee, Dr Alexandra Lewis, Chair, Adolescent Forensic Faculty Special Interest Group, Royal College of Psychiatrists, stated:

'Previously, it was thought that the most significant period of brain maturation was in the first five or possibly eight years. We now know that a second critical period takes place in adolescence and is a very dramatic development of the frontal lobes, which are, essentially, responsible for decision making, planning, consequential thinking, getting ideas about ourselves and social interaction... We have reached a point where nobody is saying any different, and everybody understands that brains are not mature by the age of 10. They are not mature by the age of 13 or 15. It is a

much longer process than anybody thought, so it does not make sense to treat somebody at 10 the same as an adult, because they are fundamentally quite different in their decision-making abilities.'

REASON 7: Criminalising children doesn't work – it does more harm than good

In asking whether a low age of criminal responsibility is in the child's best interests it is necessary to look at the impact of criminalisation on the child's future development. Research demonstrates that criminalisation of children tends to increase their risk of engaging in offending behaviour. It also stigmatises the child and alienates them from society, creates problems of self-esteem and creates barriers in the way of return to education or future employment, not least in the form of acquiring a criminal record. Punitive measures increase the likelihood of reoffending.

REASON 8: There are better ways to deal with it – better for children and better for communities

A key issue in deciding on the age of criminal responsibility is what we want the aim of the process to be. If the aim is to prevent offending, to encourage rehabilitation and the reintegration of the child into playing a constructive role in society then dealing with the child through the criminal justice system does not offer the best chance of success. Our reoffending rates demonstrate this. Government figures from the Department of Justice, reveal that the one year proven re-offending rate of young people for

- Custody release was 16 out of 20 young people
- Non-custodial disposal with supervision was 45.6%
- Non-custodial disposal without supervision was 38.6%
- Diversionary disposal was 21.5%

Rather the focus should be on assessing the child's problems and needs and attempting to meet those needs. In a children's rights compliant approach, children in conflict with the law are defined as 'children in need' and the responsibility of children's services (e.g. education, health, social care). The emphasis is on care, protection and diversion from the criminal justice system through providing support to families and helping them to access services and support. In a rights-based environment the emotional and mental health issues can be addressed without labelling the child as criminal or putting an already vulnerable child through the justice system.

This type of approach would focus more on the well-being and rehabilitation of the child; it will address the difficulties the young person has experienced which led to them becoming involved in the justice system. It will also ensure less children end up in the justice system. It is a more effective approach and will lead to better outcomes for children and families and safer communities for all.

It is also worth noting that there is a fiscal cost to the criminalisation of children and in particular to the detention of children, money which could be diverted to community alternatives. The most recent CJI inspection of Woodlands outlined that with the small number of admissions and no change in the number of staffed places, the cost of holding a young person in custody during 2020-21 was £190,206 (expressed as the cost per place including corporate overheads) or £829,988 when expressed as the cost per occupant.

Younger children who are engaged in criminal activity should be supported to realise the consequences of their behaviour. We are not suggesting that no action should be taken, nor are we condoning unacceptable behaviour. The voices of communities and specifically victims cannot be ignored and are central to this discussion. It is vital that we listen to what communities are telling us and find ways to address issues of concern. As the Youth Justice Review stated, it is not a case of whether children should be held accountable, but how they are held accountable. The evidence tells us that solutions for these issues are rarely found in criminalising very young children but in non-criminal justice interventions such as, community development, universal family support and early intervention and prevention services. Such interventions would also recognise that many children who display unacceptable behaviour have in fact been victims themselves. This connection was recognised by some respondents to the consultation in Scotland to raise the age of criminal responsibility. Proposals to increase the age of criminal responsibility in Scotland were broadly welcomed by victims' groups due to the close link between childhood victimisation and offending.

REASON 9: We can ensure our children are not in the justice system

Raising the age of criminal responsibility would remove a considerable number of children from the justice system. According to government figures, there were 456 individual children aged 10-15 years old referred to the Youth Justice Agency Services in 2021/2022.

The age breakdown of that group is as follows:

- 10-13 years old – 154 children
- 14 years old - 135 children
- 15 years old – 167 children

It is also concerning that we are seeing an increase in the numbers of 10-13 year olds coming into contact with the criminal justice system. The proportion of individual children referred to Youth Justice Agency Services aged 10-13 has increased, to account for 17% in 2021/2022, which is a considerable increase from 12% in 2017/2018. The proportion of individual children referred to Youth Justice Agency Services aged 14 has also increased, to account for 14.9% in 2021/2022, which is a considerable increase from 10.9% in 2017/2018.

In terms of individual children in custody in 2021/2022, 10-15 years old account for 42% of under 18 years old detained in Woodlands Juvenile Justice Centre. The age breakdown for this group in 2021/2022 is as follows:

- 10-13 years old – 4 children
- 14 years old – 13 children
- 15 years old – 27 children

It is worth noting that in 2021/2022 the proportion of admissions to the Juvenile Justice Centre involving children subject to Care Orders has increased from 30.9% in 2019/2020 to 37.2% in 2021/2022. Of the 106 individual children in custody in 2021/2022, 33 were subject to a Care Order and 3 were Voluntary Accommodated. The increase in care experienced children being deprived of their liberty is deeply concerning.

One in three children detained are care experienced.

Also worthy of note is the breakdown of the average population in the Juvenile Justice Centre by status. Very few children who are detained there have actually been sentenced. In 2021/2022, there were NO admissions to the Juvenile Justice under sentence, 79.7% admissions were under PACE and 20.3% were on remand.

When we look at PSNI figures for children being given Community Resolution Notices (CRNs) we see that there are a considerable number of under 16 year olds receiving these disposals: In 2018/2019, 870 CRNs were given to 10-15 year olds. There were 1,057 10-15 year old children recorded as having received prosecutions at court and out of court disposals in 2021.

REASON 10: The call for change is growing

There are increasing calls for and growing evidence to support an increase in the minimum age of criminal responsibility in NI.

- In a 2016 a Kids Life and Times survey of over 5,000 children aged 10–11 years in Northern Ireland revealed support for increasing the age of criminal responsibility. 59% of the children supported the minimum age of criminal responsibility being raised with the majority supporting an increase to 14 or 16 years old.

- The Northern Ireland Human Rights Commission has called for urgent action to address the low minimum age of criminal responsibility in Northern Ireland.

- There have been calls to raise the age of criminal responsibility to 16 years by the NI Children's Commissioner.

- The demand for change in NI has been further fuelled by the changes that have been evident in other jurisdictions, notably Scotland.

- In 2015 a number of organisations came together to form 'Raise the Age' coalition, a campaign to raise the age of criminal responsibility in NI.

- The number of voluntary agencies adding their voices to the call to raise the age has since grown and now includes Include Youth, NIACRO, Children's Law Centre, Barnardo's, Extern, NI Alternatives, Northern Ireland Youth Forum, VOYPIC, Children in NI, Parenting NI, NICVA, and Quakers Service.

- In November 2021, we launched a commissioned research report by Dr Nicola Carr and Dr Siobhan McAlister examining developments in youth justice between 2011 and 2021. The Tracing the Review report recommended that urgent action be taken to raise the age of criminal responsibility to 16 years.

November 2022

www.includeyouth.org

Boy, 5, accused of stalking and dozens of under 10s suspected of rape

Soaring numbers of crimes are being committed by children under 10, new data has shown.

By Kirsten Robertson

Five-year-olds have been investigated for stalking, four-year-olds for theft and children younger than 10 have been accused of child porn offences.

A staggering 34,000 crimes have been carried out over the last decade by those too young to be prosecuted.

New data, released by 25 police forces, shows under 10s are also accused of serious crimes such as rape and drug offences.

As 10 is the age of criminal responsibility in England and Wales, the suspects cannot be charged with committing a criminal offence.

The figures warn that child crime is a growing problem in Britain, with 4,729 crimes being committed in 2021 – up from 3,815 in 2020 and 4,447 in 2019.

Solicitor Laurence Lee, who represented 10-year-old Jon Venables in the James Bulger case, believes the reality is probably even worse than the numbers suggest.

Mr Lee, based in Liverpool, said: 'I think these numbers are underestimating it, to be honest. Youth crime is on the up unfortunately.

'It's a very sad reflection on society.

'What's the answer? Education? I don't know the answer.

Unfortunately parts of society are a cancer and are beyond help.

'The vast majority of children are good, but unfortunately they are drowned out by the minority.'

The data, obtained via Freedom of Information (FOI) requests shows urban areas see significantly more crime than rural areas.

The figures show serious crimes are being committed.

In Essex, a total of 32 under 10s were suspected of rape in 2021 – and one was even accused of drug trafficking.

Shockingly, Derbyshire Police revealed that a five year old was suspected of stalking in 2021.

In Manchester, 43 suspects under 10 were accused of child porn offences.

When responding to the FOI request, the Met Police said 55 sex offences were committed by children in 2021 – 45 by boys and 10 by girls.

The most common crime across all forces was violence without injury, while crimes like shoplifting and criminal damage were also frequent offences.

Mr Lee believes every case could be treated differently.

'You'll find that a lot of kids under 10, knowing they can't be prosecuted, are doing the dirty work for drug dealers and other criminals', he claimed.

'A lot of people say it [the age of criminal responsibility] should be raised to 12. Well, if it had been raised to 12, the Bulger killers couldn't have been prosecuted.'

Twenty five police forces out of 45 provided data when asked to under the Freedom of Information act by the Solent News Agency.

14 February 2023

Where saw the most youth crime?

In 2021 Greater Manchester Police dealt with more offences than any other force – 773 – while Dorset Police dealt with the fewest, eight.

Essex Police reported the second most offences in 2021, with 554, followed by Lancashire Constabulary with 496, then the Met Police with 408.

The fewest were in rural Dorset, with Dorset Police reporting just eight. Cheshire Constabulary reported 11 and Bedfordshire Police reported 61.

Half of ethnic minority Britons lack confidence in police to deal with local crime

A further two in five say crime in their local area has increased over the last few years.

By Tanya Abraham

New YouGov research shows that there is currently little faith among ethnic minority Britons in the police to deal with local crime, with half saying they don't have much (31%) or any confidence (19%). Around two in five have either a lot (5%) or a fair (33%) level of confidence.

Half (53%) of Asian respondents of Indian, Pakistani or Bangladeshi heritage possess little to no faith in the police locally, compared to 41% of Black respondents.

This lack of faith in the police force coincides with 41% overall saying that crime has gone up in their local area in recent

How much confidence do ethnic minority Britons have in the police to tackle crime locally?

Generally speaking, how much confidence do you have in the police to deal with crime in your local area?

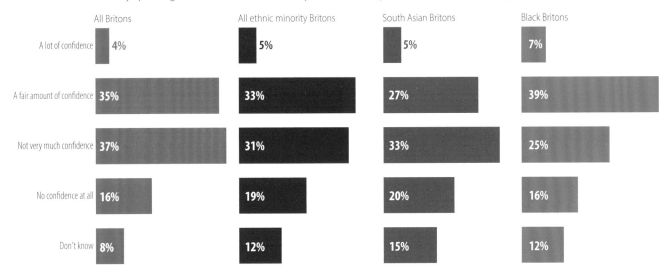

South Asian Britons are those with an Indian, Pakistani, or Bangladeshi heritage

Source: YouGov - All Britons survey: 8-10 April 2023 / Ethnic minority survey: 30 March - 12 April 2023

Ethnic minority Britons are less likely to believe that crime has gone up nationally than the public as a whole

Do you think the level of crime NATIONALLY has gone up or down over the last few years, or has it stayed the same?

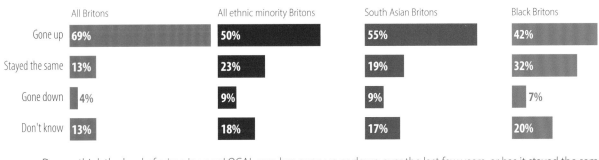

Do you think the level of crime in your LOCAL area has gone up or down over the last few years, or has it stayed the same?

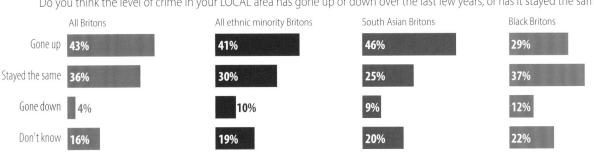

South Asian Britons are those with an Indian, Pakistani, or Bangladeshi heritage

Source: YouGov - All Britons survey: 8-10 April 2023 / Ethnic minority survey: 30 March - 12 April 2023

How do the top national issues for ethnic minority Britons compare with the wider population?

Which of the following do you think are the most important issues facing the country at this time?

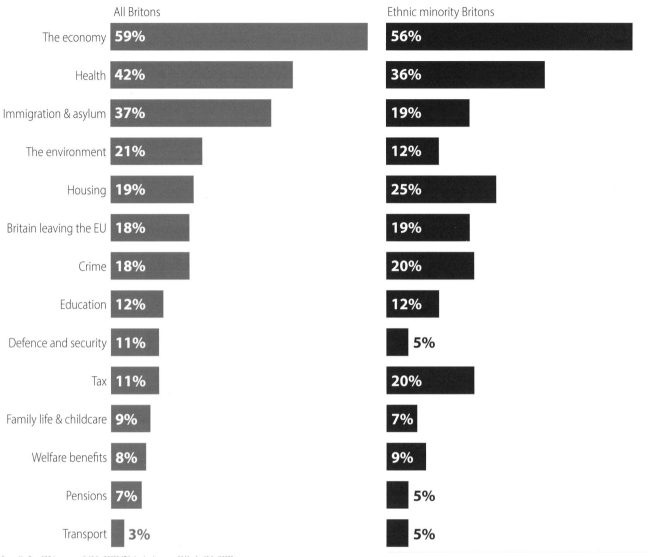

	All Britons	Ethnic minority Britons
The economy	59%	56%
Health	42%	36%
Immigration & asylum	37%	19%
The environment	21%	12%
Housing	19%	25%
Britain leaving the EU	18%	19%
Crime	18%	20%
Education	12%	12%
Defence and security	11%	5%
Tax	11%	20%
Family life & childcare	9%	7%
Welfare benefits	8%	9%
Pensions	7%	5%
Transport	3%	5%

Source: YouGov - All Britons survey: 8-10 April 2023 / Ethnic minority survey: 30 March - 12 April 2023

years. Three in ten (30%) think it has remained consistent while only 10% say it has gone down.

A further 50% also think crime has increased nationally over the last few years. A quarter (23%) believe it has stayed the same while 9% think it has fallen.

According to national tracker data, ethnic minority Britons are much less likely to think crime has risen than the wider population, 69% of whom think that crime across the country has gone up in recent years. When it comes to perceptions of crime locally, opinion among the wider public is similar to the ethnic minority population, with 43% thinking crime has increased in their local area.

Crime has grown in importance as a national issue for ethnic minority Britons: as of mid-April one in five (20%) considered this an important issue, an increase of eight points since December 2022. This is tied fourth with tax (20%) but follows the economy (56%), health (36%) and housing (25%).

On a national level, 18% of all Britons consider crime an important issue, again falling far behind many other areas such as the economy (59%), health (42%), immigration (37%) and the environment (21%).

15 May 2023

Research

Create a questionnaire to find out people's confidence in the police. How do your results compare to the survey in this article. Consider the differences in age-groups and by gender.

www.yougov.co.uk

A short guide to the criminal justice system

An extract.

Key Actors

Police forces

Police forces are responsible for the prevention, detection and investigation of crime. As such, they are also the first point of contact for anyone wishing to report a crime.

During a criminal investigation, police officers have various common law and statutory powers designed to help them gather evidence, interview people and detain suspects. They also have the power to make charging decisions in certain, lower-level cases. Police forces have an obligation to conduct effective investigations and to treat victims and witnesses in accordance with their rights.

Police and Crime Commissioners (PCCs)

Most police forces in England and Wales are overseen by an elected PCC. PCCs are also responsible for commissioning the majority of local support services for victims of crime in conjunction with their local police forces.

PCCs set their policing agenda for their area through a five-year 'police and crime plan' and will often outline their approach to victim support in these plans.

In Greater Manchester, West Yorkshire and Greater London the role of a PCC is performed by the Combined Authority Mayor. In the City of London, it is performed by the City of London Police Authority.

Crown Prosecution Service (CPS)

The primary criminal prosecuting authority in England and Wales is the CPS. The CPS is an independent body responsible for prosecuting criminal cases that have been investigated by the police and other investigative organisations.

The CPS employs criminal solicitors who can provide legal advice to the police, are often responsible for making the decision to charge a suspect and support barristers presenting the case for the prosecution in court.

The CPS is led by the Director of Public Prosecutions who is currently Max Hill QC.

Her Majesty's Courts and Tribunals Service (HMCTS)

HMCTS is the executive agency responsible for the administration of courts and tribunals in England and Wales.

HMCTS is responsible for some practical aspects of criminal court proceedings. For example, they are responsible for the safe and secure accommodation of defendants held in custody whilst they appear in court as well as the provision of courtroom adjustments afforded to vulnerable victims under the Victims' Code.

Magistrates' courts and the Crown Court

These are the courts of first instance in England and Wales, meaning that defendants will have their cases heard in one of these courts first. All cases begin at a magistrate's court but serious offences are immediately sent to the Crown Court for sentencing or trial.

Important to note is that a jury trial will only take place where a defendant pleads not guilty in the Crown Court. A defendant appealing a decision from a magistrate's court will typically do so in the Crown Court.

Court of Appeal

The Criminal Division of the Court of Appeal hears appeals of decisions from the Crown Court from the defence if they can establish grounds to appeal.

Alternatively, the Attorney General can appeal a sentence if they believe it is unduly lenient.

Depending on whether the appellant is appealing the conviction or the sentence, the Court of Appeal can amend or overturn the conviction or change the sentence as they judge necessary.

Court of Appeal Criminal Division judgments are binding on the Crown Court and magistrates' courts.

Sentencing Council

The Sentencing Council is a non-departmental, independent body that issues guidelines on sentencing in England and Wales. Its main aim is to promote greater transparency and consistency in sentencing, while maintaining the independence of the judiciary.

Reporting and Investigation

Reporting a crime

Crimes can be reported to the police in several ways:

- Dial 999 in an emergency or when reporting terrorist activity;

- Non-emergencies can be reported online or by calling 101;

- Police forces also often have their own crime reporting webpages such as Greater Manchester Police and Cambridgeshire;

- People can also report crimes anonymously to Crimestoppers, who will pass the report to the police.

Anyone can report crime to the police. Once the report is received, the police have responsibilities to provide the victim with certain information including:

- written confirmation of the crime report;

- a crime reference number;

- contact details for the police officer dealing with your case;

- details of next steps;

- how frequently the police will provide updates on the investigation.

Under their obligations in the Victim's Code, the police will carry out a 'needs assessment' to find out what support the victim requires and ask a support organisation to contact them within 2 days.

Police investigation

The first stage of any police investigation of a crime report is an initial investigation. This determines whether a full investigation would be an appropriate use of police resources. Most police forces have internal policies that guide their initial assessment decisions. For example, the Metropolitan Police 'investigative assessment' will broadly assess:

- the victim's vulnerability as defined by the Victim's Code;

- the severity of the offence;

- the case's solvability based on the evidence that exists to help build a case. For instance, are there witnesses or is CCTV evidence available?

To conclude an initial investigation, the police will need to complete various steps, including:

- obtaining an account from the victim and any other victim/s or witnesses;

- meeting the immediate needs of the victims and witnesses;

- examining the crime scene (if applicable);

- taking any fast-track actions likely to establish important facts, preserve evidence or lead to the early resolution of the investigation.

At the end of the initial investigation, the case will either be closed or allocated for further investigation.

Closing a case

Where an investigation is closed it will not be investigated further. However, if the police receive new evidence relating to the case they may decide to reopen the case. The victim and any recorded witnesses will be notified if that happens.

Further investigation and arrests

When a case is referred for further investigation, investigating officers will be assigned to the case. One officer will be assigned as the single point of contact for the victim throughout the investigation. Forces have different policies on how victim care is delivered, but victims are guaranteed access to services outlined in the Victim's Code.

If the investigation does not uncover enough evidence to charge a suspect with an offence, police have a responsibility to take 'no further action' and close the case until new evidence comes to light.

If a suspect is identified, the police have a range of investigative strategies for dealing with that individual. Suspects must be detained, treated and questioned in line with Code C of the Police and Criminal Evidence (PACE) Act 1984.

Once arrested, suspects are granted rights including being informed of the offence they have been arrested for, free legal advice and medical assistance if required.

Charging and prosecution

Where there is a realistic prospect of conviction, the police, a prosecuting authority or a private entity can make the decision to charge the suspect. This is typically the Crown Prosecution Service (CPS) but other agencies also have statutory prosecution powers.

Police charging decisions

For lower-level offences, the police can charge a suspect directly. This includes for:

- any summary offence (including criminal damage with a value of less than £5000);

- any offence of retail theft (shoplifting) or attempted retail theft provided that can be sentenced in a magistrates' court; and

- any either way offence where the defendant is likely to plead guilty and is suitable for sentence in a magistrates' court.

CPS/Public prosecution decisions

The Code for Crown Prosecutors, issued by the Director of Public Prosecutions, sets out the general principles public prosecutors should follow when they make decisions on cases.

To start or continue a public prosecution, prosecutors must ensure that the case has passed the Full Code Test. This test has two limbs:

- Evidential test - is there sufficient evidence to provide a realistic prospect of conviction against each suspect on each charge?

- Public Interest Test - is a prosecution in the public interest? Factors include the seriousness of the offence, the suspect's level of culpability and the level of harm caused. In some cases it may be more appropriate to deal with the case by way of an out-of-court disposal rather than a prosecution.

This test is used together with guidance issued by the director of Public Prosecutions.

Out of court disposals

To save time and resources for the police and courts, the police can avoid instigating a formal prosecution for some low-level offending by using an Out of Court Disposal (OOCD).

OOCDs are a range of options available to police as an alternative to prosecution. They include:

- Simple Caution - there are separate guidelines on the use of simple cautions for adult offenders and young offenders;

- Conditional caution - As with simple cautions, there are separate guidelines for youth conditional cautions;

- Penalty Notices for Disorders (PNDs) - Information on GOV.UK may be useful for constituents in understanding how and when PNDs are issued;

- Cannabis warnings - the GOV.UK drug penalties page summarises that police can issue fines or warnings for possession of cannabis. Sentencing Council guidelines may be useful for constituents who are given a cannabis warning to understand the status of the warning.

The Police, Crime, Sentencing and Courts Bill currently going through Parliament contains amendments to the adult OOCD framework which may alter the situation for constituents subject to OOCDs in the future.

The court system

Criminal cases are heard in either a magistrates' court or the Crown Court. Cases with defendants between 10-17 years-old are heard in a youth court, which are set up similarly to a magistrates' court.

Almost all cases begin in the magistrates' court which then decides whether to send the case to the Crown Court. Offences are split into three categories based on their seriousness:

Summary offences

Lower-level offences that carry lesser sentences, such as most motoring offences or minor criminal damage. They are usually dealt with by a magistrates' court, but the Crown Court can deal with summary offences in certain circumstances.

Either-way offences

Offences that can be sentenced in either a magistrates' court or Crown Court such as burglary and many drug offences.

Indictable offences

Serious offences that can only be tried 'on indictment' in the Crown Court, such as robbery or serious violent or sexual offences. Cases are typically sent to the Crown Court immediately on an initial hearing.

If a defendant pleads guilty to the offence as charged, the case will move immediately to sentencing. In a magistrates' court, the defendant may be sentenced immediately or referred to the Crown Court for sentencing at a later date if the offence is sufficiently serious.

Where a defendant pleads not guilty, the case will go to trial. Here, the prosecution will present their case for a conviction and the defendant will have an opportunity to refute that case.

Court proceedings and appearing in court

All trials in England and Wales are conducted in accordance with the Criminal Procedure Rules, which govern every aspect of every stage of the criminal court process.

If the case is being heard in a magistrates' court, the trial will be overseen by two or three magistrates or a District Judge. Trials for offences in magistrates' courts are known as summary trials.

A trial in the Crown Court will be held with a jury who is guided throughout the case by the judge before reaching a verdict on the defendant's guilt. Juries are constituted of 12 people randomly selected from the electoral register.

Parties to the case can sometimes vet or object to selection of members of the jury. More details on this process and the different types of judges are published on the Judiciary website.

Evidence and witnesses

The parties build their cases around sources of evidence including forensics and witnesses.

In the interests of a fair trial and the principle of 'equality of arms', strict disclosure rules ensure that both parties have access to evidence that may undermine the case for the prosecution.

Police and prosecutors are obligated to treat witnesses in accordance with the Witness Charter and victim witness in accordance with enhanced rights granted by the Victim's Code.

Further information on the Victim's Code is published in the Library's constituency casework article on support for victims.

Staying proceedings

At any point, the court has the power to halt or 'stay' proceedings where it believes there has been an abuse of process that would undermine a defendant's right to a fair trial if proceedings were allowed to continue.

11 January 2022

www.parliament.uk

UK courts explained

In this article, we will discuss which courts supersede which and what all the different courts address. Here are the UK Courts explained.

By Michael Coyle

Here is a brief overview of the UK court system and UK Courts explained:

County Courts: The County Courts are the lowest level of courts in the UK, dealing with civil claims such as debt recovery, contract disputes, and personal injury claims. They also handle some minor criminal cases, such as traffic offences and minor assaults.

High Court: The High Court is the next level up from the County Courts and deals with more complex civil claims and serious criminal cases. There are three divisions of the High Court: the Queen's Bench Division, the Chancery Division, and the Family Division.

Court of Appeal: The Court of Appeal is the second highest court in the UK and hears appeals from the High Court and some lower courts.

Supreme Court: The Supreme Court is the highest court in the UK and hears appeals from the Court of Appeal and other lower courts. It also acts as the final court of appeal for some cases from Scotland and Northern Ireland.

Crown Courts: The Crown Courts handle serious criminal cases, such as murder, rape, and robbery. They also hear appeals from the Magistrates' Courts.

Magistrates' Courts: The Magistrates' Courts deal with minor criminal cases, such as traffic offences and minor assaults. They also handle some civil cases, such as debt recovery and landlord-tenant disputes.

UK's Court System – additional courts

In addition to these courts, there are also specialist courts that deal with specific types of cases, such as the Employment Tribunal for employment disputes and the Intellectual Property Enterprise Court for intellectual property disputes.

It's important to note that the court system in the UK is separate from the legal profession. Judges are appointed based on their legal knowledge and experience, and are independent from the government and other parties involved in the case.

I hope this helps give you a better understanding of the UK court system!

UK's Court System History

The history of the courts in England and Wales dates all the way back to the Middle Ages. However, the Judicature Acts of 1873 and 1875 set up the modern judicial system.

The common law courts and the equity courts made up two distinct legal systems in England and Wales prior to the passage of these statutes. As a result, matters frequently had to be tried in both systems, which caused confusion and inefficiency in the judicial system.

A unified system of courts was created by the Judicature Acts of 1873 and 1875 by combining the common law and equity courts. As a result, matters could be tried in a single court by judges who were knowledgeable in both common law and equity, creating a more streamlined and effective legal system.

The English and Welsh courts are currently organised into two primary divisions: civil and criminal. The criminal courts deal with matters involving alleged criminal offences, whereas the civil courts handle disputes between people, businesses, and other organisations.

The County Court, the High Court, and the Court of Appeal are the additional three divisions of the civil courts. The Magistrates' Court, the Crown Court, and the Court of Appeal are the three layers of the criminal courts.

The English and Welsh judicial systems are now considered among the most effective and efficient in the world, and they are essential to maintaining the rule of law and defending the rights of people and corporations.

4 April 2023

Jury service

Performing jury service is an important civic duty, but it can interfere with work and daily life. A set of rules outlines the required behaviour during jury service, when jury service can be deferred or avoided, and what people will be paid by their employers or the courts whilst doing jury service.

What is jury service?

Juries

Some court cases will use a jury to help determine the outcome of a criminal trial (or, very occasionally, a civil court case). A jury is a panel of 12 (in England and Wales) or 15 (in Scotland) members of the public who must vote on whether or not the defendant (the person accused of committing a crime) in the case is guilty of the alleged offence. The jury is presented with evidence and told about relevant law by the judge. They can discuss the case amongst themselves (alone, in the jury room) and then they must vote - often the vote has to be unanimous. A jury is not required to explain their reasoning to the court or anybody else.

Jury service

Members of the public are chosen at random from the electoral register and summoned to (ie told to come to) court to complete their jury service (ie to be a part of a jury). Jury service will usually last for 10 days but can last longer.

If you've been selected to do jury service, you will receive a letter telling you that you have been chosen (this is known as a 'jury summons' in England and Wales or a 'jury citation' in Scotland). In England and Wales, you must respond to the summons within 7 days of receiving it. The courts will then send you details on when and where you must complete your jury service. For more information, read the Government's guidance and the Scottish Government's guidance.

Jury service rules

Jury members must abide by strict rules on talking about the trial that they are a part of. Prohibited practices include:

* discussing the trial outside of the jury room before the end of the trial

* discussing the deliberations that take place in the jury room

* discussing the trial on social media

Doing any of these things could constitute contempt of court.

Do I have to do jury service?

Completing jury service is an important civic duty and you cannot simply refuse to do it. Failing to answer a jury summons without reasonable cause can be a criminal offence. You can, however, apply to defer (ie delay) or be excused from your jury service.

Doing jury service whilst knowingly being ineligible for, not qualified for or disqualified from jury service can also be an offence in Scotland. For example, this may be the case if you don't meet the age or residency requirements or you hold a particular professional role (eg you are a police officer or a solicitor).

Deferring jury service in England and Wales

If you have a good reason why you cannot do jury service on the dates that you have been summoned for, you can apply to defer your service to another date within the next 12 months. Possible 'good reasons' include (but are not limited to):

* becoming a parent

* taking a holiday which you have already booked

* taking an exam

* attending an important medical appointment or an operation

* your employer will not allow you time off work

To change the date of your jury service, request this when you reply to your jury summons. For more information, read the Government's guidance.

Being excused from jury service in England and Wales

In exceptional circumstances (ie for more than just a 'good reason'), you may be excused from jury service. This may be appropriate if you cannot do jury service at any time within the next 12 months. You may need to provide evidence of your reasons for being excused (eg a letter from your GP). Exceptional circumstances include (but are not limited to):

* you or somebody that you're a carer for has an illness or injury which prevents you from being able to do jury service

* you're a new parent and cannot do jury service at any time in the next 12 months because of this

You may also be excused from jury service if you have already done jury service within the last 2 years.

Excusal from jury service in Scotland

You can apply for excusal from jury service in Scotland for various reasons.

You can usually be excused 'as of right' if you apply within 7 days to be excused and you fit within certain categories (eg you're a registered medical professional or a serving member of the armed forces).

It's also possible to apply for excusal on grounds of ill health or physical disability. You must submit evidence with your application, for example a letter from your GP.

You can also apply for excusal due to 'other special reasons', if for example you have work commitments the cancellation of which would seriously inconvenience you or others, or you have pre-arranged holiday plans which would be expensive or difficult to alter.

The 12-month deferral rule does not apply in Scotland as it does in England and Wales. When you apply for excusal, you should let the courts know if, for example, you have a medical condition preventing you from doing jury service which is long-term and unlikely to change, so that this can be taken into account.

Do employers have to grant time off work for jury service?

Employers must let their employees do jury service if they are summoned. If they do not, employees in England and Wales may complain to an Employment Tribunal. If an employee is dismissed because they do jury service, this may be unfair dismissal. However, employers can ask employees to defer or apply for excusal from their jury service if their leaving to do jury service would seriously harm the business. The employer must write a letter explaining the circumstances, which the employee must send when they respond to their jury summons.

Employers can only request that an employee's jury service is deferred once during a 12 month period. Employers must also ensure that they don't treat their employees in any way which could count as discrimination due to their taking time off work to do jury service.

Do I get paid during jury service?

Employers do not have to pay employees while they are doing jury service. However, employees (and self-employed people and people receiving benefits) may be able to obtain a certain amount of reimbursement from the courts. To clearly communicate your chosen approach to employees' pay whilst they are undertaking jury service, you can create a Jury service policy.

Allowances and expenses in England and Wales

If they're not paid by their employer during jury service, employees can claim a loss of earnings allowance and reimbursement for other expenses from the courts (ie some transport, childcare, and food and drink costs). These amounts differ depending on factors like how many hours you spend in court each day.

To claim childcare, food and drink, and travel expenses, employees must fill in various forms and return them to the courts. To claim for loss of earnings, their employer must fill in a 'loss of earnings form'.

There are similar provisions for claiming expenses if you're self-employed or not working.

Employers may choose to top up employees' loss of earnings allowances so that they don't miss out on pay when doing jury service. To do so, they must fill in a loss of earnings form (as they would if they were not paying their employees during jury service) and employees must submit the form. They should then pay employees the difference between the amount they receive from the courts and their normal take-home pay. Employers may also choose to partially top up their employees' pay, so that they are effectively being paid some (eg 90%) of their normal pay.

Allowances in Scotland

Jury members in Scotland can apply for 6 different types of allowance to make up for the expenses they incurred to undertake jury service. The allowances are for:

- loss of earnings (to a maximum of either your usual take-home pay or the maximum allowance limits set by the courts)
- travel to and from court
- subsistence (eg for food you purchased whilst attending court)
- loss of benefits (if your benefits are withdrawn during your jury service)
- childminding or dependent adult carer expenses (beyond your usual expenses)
- other expenses (you should discuss any other expenses you think you should be reimbursed for with the clerk of court)

To claim these allowances you should use a claims form and/or a certificate of loss of earnings/benefit form.

23 May 2023

Is prison an effective form of punishment?

By Cara Fielder

ULaw Criminology Lecturer Angela Charles completed her BA undergraduate degree in History and Criminology, followed by an MSc in Criminology and Criminal Justice. She is currently completing a PhD which explores the experiences of Black women in UK prisons through an intersectional lens. Her studies focus on the unique impact race and gender has on black female prisoners. Angela has worked within the criminal justice sector in a Secure Training Centre, the National Probation Service, and Youth Justice. Today Angela answers the question – is prison an effective form of punishment?

How do we assess the effectiveness of prisons?

Reform

Reform is arguably one of the most important reasons why prisons are vital. The gov.uk website talks about providing the right services and opportunities that support rehabilitation to prevent a return to crime. Some of the areas they mention are:

- Improving prisoners' mental health and tackling substance misuse

- Improving prisoners' progress in maths and English

- Increasing the numbers of offenders in employment and accommodation after release.

I would add that offenders should also be supported in learning about money and finance, improving their confidence, developing their understanding of supportive relationships, dealing with issues that may arise or previous traumas. Reform is about equipping someone with the tools to successfully navigate life's difficulties without resorting to crime.

Life after prison is the final theme on the website and this is the support needed by prisoners once they are released. This includes working with probation services. They highlight the need for services that support prisoners from the transition 'through the gate'. The main factors being employment and accommodation. When looking at the statistics for prisons achieving their target for accommodation on the first night following release, this is only 17.3%. When we look at employment targets within the first 6 weeks of release, this was at 4%, which is very low. These statistics raise concerns as to whether prison is successful in rehabilitation. Or is it merely a punishment that puts people's lives on hold?

Real life examples of the prison being effective and ineffective

Education

One woman I interviewed explained that none of the education options in the prison were suitable. She already had a degree, so did not need the English and maths classes that were provided. To her, the prison just wanted to tick a box to show people in prison were engaging in some form of education rather than helping black women progress and gain educational skills that were tailored to an individual's needs and current level of education.

However, another Black woman said that being in prison had forced her to take level 1 and 2 English and Maths. She had been putting it off when she was in society but being in prison allowed her to take the time to do it. She passed and felt that she would have better prospects leaving the prison than when she came in. Additionally, she had been trained on how to clean up chemical spills and learnt all about the control of substances hazardous to health (COSSH). Again, she learnt new skills that she felt she would be able to use in the outside world.

Relationships

Many women stated that they could speak to their loved ones regularly on the phone, which allowed them to stay connected. However, some of the women complained about how costly phone calls were. Also, transport to the prison was an expense that many women's families could not afford. Therefore, in some cases, relationships with families were put on hold.

One woman talked about her drug recovery and explained how supportive her drug worker had been. They helped her through her recovery and were a source of support and consistency during her prison experience. Even when she moved onto another wing, she mentioned how this staff member still came to check on her. She believes if she had not come to prison, she would still be addicted to drugs. In this case, imprisonment was effective and helped her to rehabilitate.

Another example came from a woman who said that her prison experience allowed her to improve herself, deal with previous traumas, and come up with ways to deal with this. She used the prison experience to identify what things triggered previous traumas and how to deal with this, as well as living in the moment. In this sense, sometimes prison can be used as a period of reflection and self-improvement.

Racism

The final example I want to give comes from several women that highlighted the systemic racism they felt was occurring in the prison. The women stated that many of the officers stereotyped them as aggressive, loud troublemakers because of their race. This had a knock-on effect because it affected how long it took for women to get moved from a closed prison to an open prison, be released for day visits, to work and see family. It also meant that they felt like they could not be themselves. For these women, prison was not effective because they were dealing with the disadvantage of being black and female. They had fewer opportunities for employment progression and they had few supportive relationships with staff. When we think about examples like this, we must determine how effective the prison would be for these women. It would be a punishment but would it help rehabilitate them or leave them bitter, angry, frustrated and no better off than before they entered the prison?

Criminological arguments for prisons

One argument for prison is that it is an effective deterrent. Prison can be seen as a tough type of punishment because it takes away your freedom, potential support networks and in many ways, it strips away your identity. The thought of prison is enough for some people to not even contemplate committing a criminal act.

Prison sentences are also a message to the wider public that this is what will happen if you commit a crime. Prison advocates would say this is a message to wider society about what is right and wrong and what will happen if you commit a crime.

Additionally, prison advocates argue that prison is such a difficult time for people that the experience should then deter them from committing any further offences. However, we know that is not the case because many individuals who have committed an offence and go to prison then commit further offences. This makes us question, is prison a) effective and b) enough of a deterrence?

Another argument for prison is that by putting people in prison, we protect the public by ensuring these individuals cannot commit any further offences. Additionally, prison sentences provide a sense of justice to the victims affected by the crime and the public.

Criminological arguments against prisons

The first argument would be that prisons do not work. Those advocating for prison reform highlight reoffending statistics as an example of the ineffectiveness of prisons.

The adult reoffending rate for the October to December 2018 cohort was 27.5%.

Almost 101,000 proven re-offences were committed over the one-year follow-up period by around 25,000 adults. Those that reoffended committed on average 3.97 re-offences. [Source – Home Office – Proven reoffending statistics for England and Wales, published October 2020].

Research shows that long prison sentences have little impact on crime. Time in prison can actually make someone more likely to commit crime — by further exposing them to all sorts of criminal elements. Prisons are also costly, using up funds that could go to other government programs that are more effective at fighting crime.

Additionally, there are arguments that prison does not rehabilitate prisoners. While there are some opportunities in prison, this does not always meet the needs of the prisoners and does not help them on their release due to the views people in society have about imprisonment and criminal records. On release, three-fifths of prisoners have no 'identified employment or education or training outcome'. If prison punishes people through the experience itself but

then does not offer those individuals the opportunity to improve and change their lives once they are released, can we realistically expect people to be rehabilitated and not return to crime?

Some believe that the whole prison system is an oppressive institution governed by the powerful that cages the marginalised and powerless. They would argue that prison further damages people because it causes further trauma, exposes them to further violence, reinforces disadvantage and creates further crime and social harm. The prison also does very little to tackle the underlying causes of crime in communities. However, some have argued that by reducing the prison population, we are still widening the net and criminalising people, as community sentences and alternatives to custody would be increased rather than looking at some of the structural inequalities that may lead to crime and criminal behaviour.

Others argue that prison mainly holds those that are from lower socio-economic backgrounds and ethnic minorities, punishing poverty and disadvantage while protecting the crimes of the powerful. For example, where are the imprisoned individuals from corporations that cause widespread harm, such as those that need to be held accountable for the Grenfell Tower fire, multi-million corporations and so on?

There are many arguments for abolishing prison, and then there are arguments that recognise prison cannot be abolished completely but needs reforming.

The United Nations Office on Drugs and Crime highlights some of the reasons why prisons need to be reformed. These are:

- Human rights, as prison is a deprivation of the basic right to liberty.

- Imprisonment disproportionately affects individuals and families living in poverty. From the potential loss of income from an individual going to prison, lawyer costs, costs to visit and communicate with that individual, the lack of employment opportunities when released, the marginalisation and so on.

- Public health consequences – It is argued that many prisoners have poor health and existing health problems when entering the prison. These problems are exacerbated due to; overcrowding, poor nutrition, lack of exercise and fresh air. Then there are also the infection rates, self-harm and poor mental health. The argument is that staff will be vulnerable to some of these diseases, and so will the public once these individuals are released.

- Detrimental social impact – Imprisonment disrupts relationships and weakens social cohesion.

- Costs – The cost of each prisoner for their upkeep, but also the social, economic and health costs mentioned previously, which are long-term.

The Howard League for Penal Reform says on their website:

'The prison system is like a river.

The wider it gets, the faster it flows – and the harder it becomes to swim against the tide. Rather than being guided to safer shores, those in the middle are swept into deeper currents of crime, violence and despair. What began as a trickle turns into a torrent, with problems in prisons spilling into the towns and cities around them.'

In conclusion, when we think about the prison, and imprisonment as a punishment and reform option, there is a lot to consider. We need to assess the overall effectiveness of prisons and the need for justice against the harm imprisonment can have on an individual. We must consider the long-term impact the prison has on an individual, not just mentally, but also considering the impact it will have on their life chances and their ability to reintegrate into society.

25 July 2022

The above information is reprinted with kind permission from The University of Law.
© 2024 The University of Law

www.law.ac.uk

Criminal sentencing is too soft, say two-thirds of Britons

By Isabelle Kirk

A new YouGov survey reveals Britons think convicted criminals should be punished more harshly by the courts – with support for harsher punishments highest among Conservative voters and older Britons.

Our latest data shows that two thirds of Britons (65%) think that the sentences that courts hand down to people who have been convicted of crimes are not harsh enough. Just 12% think the courts get the balance right, while 2% say sentences are too harsh and 21% are unsure.

The overwhelming majority of Conservative voters (83%) say sentencing for convicted criminals is not harsh enough, and it is also the most popular choice for Labour voters, at 51%. This difference is mostly explained by a significantly higher percentage of Labour voters answering 'don't know' (30%) compared to Conservative voters (just 8%).

Britons over 65 are also much more likely to be say sentencing is not harsh enough (77%) compared to those aged 18-24 (43%). Again, however, this does not translate into younger Britons saying that sentences are too harsh or that the balance is right – more than a third (37%) of 18 to 24-year-olds are unsure about the harshness of sentencing for convicted criminals, compared to just 12% of those aged over 65.

Women are somewhat more likely than men to think that criminals are not punished harshly enough by the courts, by 69% to 61%.

30 March 2022

Two-thirds of Britons think current punishments handed out to convicted criminals are not harsh enough

Generally speaking, do you think the sentences that the courts hand down to people who have been convicted of crimes are too harsh, not harsh enough, or get the balance about right?

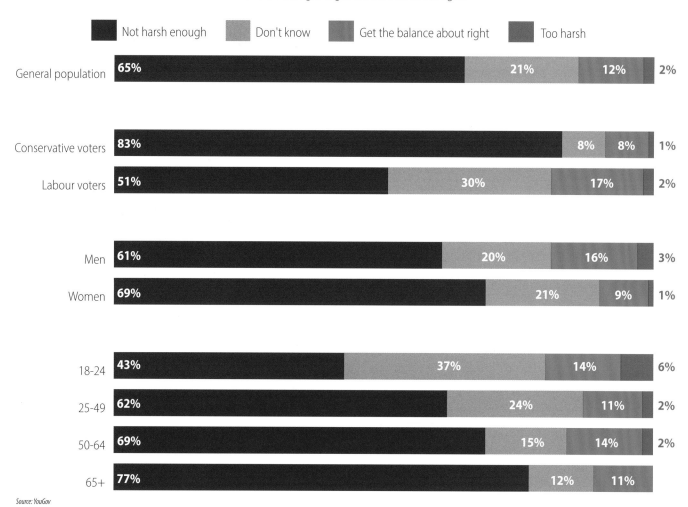

Source: YouGov

Is prison really a holiday camp?

I'd never given serious thought about what it would be like to be locked up behind bars 24/7.

By Brianna Cyrus, Programme Manager for Routes2Success by Action for Race Equality

When I was growing up, I heard the stories about 'Feltham' being like a holiday camp. To be honest, I thought there was some truth in it. I saw young men I had grown up with, one after the other enter 'Feltham' and keep going back. There was no deterrent, which made me think it must be better than life on the outside!

It wasn't until I started working at Action for Race Equality (ARE) that I got a sound understanding of how the criminal justice system works and could truly appreciate the issues and difficulties prisoners face. Not only was it an eye opener for me to talk to the men experiencing the British criminal justice system and to the prison staff but, just as important, I was working with role models who had been through it and had a positive outlook.

But the young men describing Feltham as a 'holiday camp' played over and over in my mind and hearing that many had the luxuries of televisions and computer consoles at their disposal. One of our Routes2Success role models assured me that being in any type of prison was no stroll in the park. I asked him if that was the case why so many reoffended. Surely if the experience is that bad they would stay away.

His description of what the prisoners see as a 'brotherhood' put things into perspective for me.

Imagine being on the outside, free from the restraints of an oppressive 24 hour 'bang up' regime, but having no-one or nothing. No family because your dad left when you were young and your mum worked around the clock to bring in the little money that she could. So you only had your friends from the 'endz'. Not real friends because they showed you how to 'shot' to make ends meet, steal and lie to those around you.

Then you end up behind bars and meet like-minded people. People who have been through what you have. People who understand where you are coming from and so you form that 'brotherhood'. Then the visits from your loved ones become less frequent. As the inmates from HMP Wayland in Norfolk explain, 'It's just too far to travel from London' and the expenses you incur from one visit makes it 'impossible to have regular visits'. So you get lonely and lean on your fellow inmates for support.

Added to this, you have prison staff without a clue about what it means to be a young black man; isolated and alone in Norfolk never having experienced life outside their 'all white' Norfolk village. So again you look to your brothers inside for that united front.

Years down the line and you are due for release but that all becomes daunting as you have become 'institutionalised'; used to being in this environment. Comfortable.

The prisoners at HMP Wayland and Thameside shared their fears of being released. Not being able to provide for their family, being broke, dealing with a hostile environment, mental strength, getting a job, friends. The list goes on!

All these fears are playing on their mind upon release and then they face the harsh realities when they get out. It can be overwhelming and hard to get through, especially if your ideas of a 'man' means being able to provide for your family but you are repeatedly turned down by employers.

So you turn back to what you know best and make some money which leads to you ending up back behind bars!

This is not always the only reason that these young men reoffend, but it is also going back to your comfort zone – having a roof over your head, the safety of the four walls, others who you can relate to, no one to answer to. Unlike the harsh realities of the outside world, prison can seem like a safety net.

So my opinions have changed. Prison isn't a holiday camp. Anyone who describes it as this has some harsh realities to face up to in the outside world if they think that prison is a better place to be. If a young person feels freer in prison than in the outside world we have to realise that society has to address some serious problems and that rehabilitation needs to provide the safety net that these young people need.

29 October 2021

Three-quarters of prisons in England and Wales in appalling conditions as overcrowding fears grow

Observer investigation finds system is in 'worst state ever' as senior figures warn of inmates 'being warehoused'.

By Michael Savage

The vast majority of prisons are providing inadequate conditions or unacceptable treatment, according to an Observer investigation that has led to claims of prisoners being 'warehoused' in a system in crisis.

An analysis of hundreds of inspections found that three-quarters of prisons in England and Wales are now providing insufficient standards in at least one respect.

More than a third were deemed to be insufficiently safe. On Saturday night, several senior figures warned that prisons were in the worst condition they had known.

The chief inspector of prisons, the Tory chair of the justice committee and senior prison staff all warned that the findings had been fuelled by overcrowding. The prison population stands at 86,763, with just 947 empty cells in England and Wales. However, insiders said that the supposedly 'spare' cells were often in the wrong places or inappropriate for incoming prisoners.

The news comes with instances of prison deaths, suicides and serious assaults on inmates and staff increasing. There has also been an alarming rise in the rates of self-harm in women's prisons – up 51% in the year to June.

Andrea Albutt, president of the Prison Governors Association, called for an urgent early release scheme. She said recent policies designed to hand out tougher sentences, together with crowded prisons, a backlog of remanded prisoners and a smaller, inexperienced workforce meant it was now necessary.

'We are stuffed to the gunwales,' she said. 'We are doing little more than warehousing people. The result is that we're delivering really poor regimes in many of our prisons, with prisoners locked up for 22 hours a day. In a nutshell, it's dangerous.

'This is absolutely the worst I've ever seen. They have got to look at an early release scheme of some kind … It is very straightforward. The big thing to sort out the crisis we've got is to reduce the population by thousands.'

All prisons are inspected to see if they satisfy basic standards for safety, respect for prisoners, access to purposeful activities and rehabilitation. In each area, they are deemed as being good, reasonably good, insufficiently good or poor.

The Observer examined 245 full inspections covering 123 of the prisons in operation. The most recent inspections for each prison stated that 95 were poor or not sufficient in at least one area. Two-thirds were failing to provide adequate purposeful activity.

Experts said it was a sign that prisons had failed to lift Covid measures that saw prisoners locked up for long periods. More than 40% of prisons recorded a worse score compared with their previous inspection.

Just in the last fortnight, inspectors raised the alarm over the conditions in Bristol, now regarded as one of the unsafest prisons in the country. Eight men had killed themselves since the last inspection, while one had been charged with the murder of a cellmate. Emergency cell call bells often went unanswered, and the prison was found to be 'violent and riddled with drugs'.

Charlie Taylor, the chief inspector of prisons, told the Observer: 'These worrying findings correspond closely with those of our own annual report, published last month, and with the issues that led me to write to the secretary of state issuing an urgent notification for improvement at Bristol prison.

'The situation in many institutions is concerning and, as population pressures compound this, we need to see resolute support from the centre for every prison and every prison governor. We cannot allow a situation to persist where prisoners are simply warehoused in deteriorating conditions, with the real risk of harm not only to them as

individuals but also to the public if their rehabilitation has not been supported during their time in custody.'

Bob Neill, the Tory chief of the justice select committee, said: 'It is an extremely serious situation as we are looking at a prison population which could rise above 100,000 in the next four years.

'Our own research shows that half of prison officers do not feel safe at work and more than three-quarters of those surveyed reported that morale was not good. It all points to a high-pressure environment, and the government needs to set out what measures it is taking to address this wholly unacceptable situation, both in the short and long term.'

Nick Hardwick, the former chief inspector of prisons who is now professor of criminal justice at Royal Holloway, University of London, said prisons were in 'the most dangerous state I can remember'. He added: 'The increase is not just because we are sending more people to prison but because we are sending people to prison for much longer – the taps are full on and the outflow is blocked.'

Campaigners called for the return of the end of custody licence scheme, an early release programme introduced by Labour in 2007 to deal with overcrowding. It was abolished in 2010.

'Today's government must recognise the gravity of the situation and look to a similar initiative if the prison system is to have any chance of recovery,' said Andrew Neilson, director of campaigns at the Howard League for Penal Reform.

The Ministry of Justice said the overall rate of assaults remained 23% lower than prior to the pandemic. The government said it was still committed to creating 20,000 modern prison places.

A spokesperson said: 'This government is doing more than ever to deliver safe and secure prisons that rehabilitate offenders, cut crime and protect the public. Assaults are nearly a third lower than in 2019 as a result of these efforts, and our £100 million investment in tough security measures – including X-ray body scanners – is stopping the weapons, drugs and phones that fuel violence behind bars.

'At the same time, we are pressing ahead with the biggest expansion of prison places in over a century, recruiting up to 5,000 more prison officers and creating a prisoner education service so offenders get the support and skills they need to put crime behind them.'

5 August 2023

Broken Britain: Cleaning up Cleveland, the UK's crime capital

With some of the worst violent crime rates in the country, John Johnston reports on efforts to clean up Cleveland.

With one of the highest levels of violent crime in the country and a police force in special measures, Cleveland is a frequent chart topper when it comes to identifying England's worst area for crime.

Unlike many other areas high on the list, Cleveland is unique in that it doesn't encompass a major city, with much of its population dispersed across the towns of Hartlepool, Stockton-on-Tees and Middlesbrough. But with poor economic growth and few job opportunities, the area is blighted by high levels of drug use and records more knife crime than anywhere else in the country.

Elected in May 2021, Steve Turner, the local Police and Crime Commissioner, is committed to turning round the region's shocking crime stats, something he believes is as much about economics as it is about policing.

'We've got a lot of violent crime here in Cleveland, and that includes knife crime and just general violent behaviour. The vast majority of it, when it is traced back, is drug related,' he tells The House. 'I'm told drugs are relatively cheap to buy in Tees Valley compared to the rest of the country.'

'Looking at it holistically, the economic circumstances here in Teesside have been driven down. We've lost a lot of industry and things like that, so the whole levelling up agenda is something important, because whilst it doesn't feel policing-related, I am a big believer in the fact that if you give people jobs and opportunity then that comes with less crime and more stability.'

Sitting on the boards of high street regeneration projects, lobbying ministers over levelling up and working with local businesses to fund the resurfacing of outdoor football pitches breaks what Turner believes is the common public misconception of his role, but is certain is vital to addressing Cleveland's crime rate.

'It's a bit of a chicken and egg, you can't really attract investment unless you're attracting people to an area which is safe for them and their employees to live and work in, so the levelling up piece has a big part to play in that,' he adds.

'When people look at the role, all they see is police, but the phrase I use probably the most is that I'm not Batman. When someone tags me in a Facebook post and says my son's bike was stolen, what are you going to do about it? The answer is, personally, I'm not going to come out and find the individual who took your son's bike and bring him to justice.'

To boost his work, Turner's office recently secured a £3.5 million funding package from the government aimed at reducing violent crime, both through additional policing, but crucially, through improving conditions in the community.

'When we talk about violent reduction units, it's not cops with guns, which is how the public perception of it is – it's about getting upstream of the problem. The best way to stop violent crime is for violent crime not to happen in the first place.'

Taking a carrot and stick approach, Turner insists that police will continue to clamp down on anti-social behaviour, but says he hopes offering a swathe of community projects will create opportunities for young people to avoid becoming repeat offenders.

'You've got to work with them to show there are other options, because often the role models in these children's lives are criminals. One local project we work with is a basketball club that have created their own initiative that is called 'role models'.

'That is aimed at teaching young people that there are better ways to do things. There are other options. There are other people they can look up to than the role models they currently have in their life. That sort of project really underpins a lot of the work we are doing.'

30 January 2023

Global use of death penalty at highest rate for five years

- More than a third of recorded executions were for drugs offences, a clear breach of international law

- Iran carried out a colossal 576 executions and Saudi Arabia 196, its highest number in 30 years, while China, where death penalty data is kept secret, is thought to have executed thousands

- At least 28,282 people were under sentence of death at the end of 2022

- *'James Cleverly should unequivocally call on the Chinese authorities to publish official data on China's massive use of the death penalty'* – **Sacha Deshmukh**

The number of recorded executions carried out last year reached the highest figure in five years, Amnesty International said today, as it published a global report on the death penalty.

Amnesty's 46-page report – *Death Sentences and Executions 2022*, its authoritative annual survey on the death penalty – shows that during 2022 a total of 883 people are known to have been executed across 20 countries, a rise of 53% compared to the number of executions the organisation recorded during 2021. The large spike in executions – which does not include the thousands believed to have been carried out in China last year – was the result of sharp increases in several countries in the Middle East.

Excluding China – where the authorities refuse to publish official data on the death penalty – 90% of the world's known executions last year were carried out by just three countries: Iran (576 executions, up from 314), Saudi Arabia (196 executions, up from 65) and Egypt (24 executions). The number of executions for Saudi Arabia was the highest

Amnesty has recorded in 30 years, and comes at a time when the country is investing heavily in international sporting ventures as part of a long-term sportswashing drive.

The use of the death penalty remained shrouded in secrecy in several countries, including China, North Korea, and Vietnam – countries that are known to use the death penalty extensively – meaning that the true global figure is far higher than the minimum figure recorded by Amnesty. While the precise number of those killed in China is unknown, it is nevertheless certain that the country remained the world's most prolific executioner, ahead of Iran, Saudi Arabia, Egypt and the USA. During 2022, the USA carried out 18 executions, up from 11 the previous year.

Amnesty's report also shows that executions resumed in five countries during 2022 – Afghanistan, Kuwait, Myanmar, the State of Palestine and Singapore.

While executions were up significantly during 2022, the number of recorded death sentences imposed on people remained at very nearly the same level as the previous year – with 2,016 new death sentences handed down during 2022 versus 2,052 in 2021. Globally, at least 28,282 people were under sentence of death at the end of 2022.

As of December 2022, 112 countries had abolished the death penalty for all crimes and nine countries had abolished the death penalty for ordinary crimes only.

Agnès Callamard, Amnesty International's Secretary General, said:

'Countries in the Middle East and North Africa region violated international law as they ramped up executions in 2022,

revealing a callous disregard for human life.

'The number of individuals deprived of their lives rose dramatically across the region; Saudi Arabia executed a staggering 81 people in a single day.

'Most recently, in a desperate attempt to end the popular uprising, Iran executed people simply for exercising their right to protest.

'It's time for governments and the UN to up the pressure on those responsible for these blatant human rights violations and ensure international safeguards are put in place.'

China's executions and UK diplomacy

Though the Chinese authorities refuse to release information relating to their use of the death penalty, based on its monitoring Amnesty believes that the number of death sentences imposed and executions carried out in China during 2022 was – as in previous years – in the thousands. Economic crimes, such as corruption – which do not meet the threshold of the 'most serious crimes' under international law and standards – are punishable by death in China.

Sacha Deshmukh, Amnesty International UK's Chief Executive, said:

'The UK government regularly restates its formal "opposition" to the death penalty but what is it actually doing to actively end its use in places like Iran, Saudi Arabia, Egypt or China?

'When the Foreign Secretary says we should "engage" with China, in what way – if it all – can he point to the UK engaging with officials in Beijing over China's appalling execution death toll?

'At the very least, James Cleverly should unequivocally call on the Chinese authorities to publish official data on China's massive use of the death penalty, a deadly practice which is currently totally shrouded in secrecy.

'Opposition to the calculated cruelty of the death penalty requires well-resourced, human rights–focused UK diplomacy, and we're increasingly concerned that the Government's prioritisation of trade and security is undermining its efforts on human rights.'

Executions carried out during 2022

- China: unknown but believed to be thousands
- Iran: 576
- Saudi Arabia: 196
- Egypt: 24
- USA: 18
- Iraq: 11+
- Singapore: 11
- Kuwait: 7
- Somalia: 6+
- South Sudan: 5+
- Palestine: 5
- Yemen: 4+
- Bangladesh: 4
- Myanmar: 4
- Belarus: 1
- Japan: 1

The following countries are known to have carried out executions although the actual number is unknown: Afghanistan, North Korea, Syria and Vietnam.

An + symbol indicates that the number is a minimum one and that it is likely that other executions also took place.

Executions for drugs offences more than double

The recorded number of people executed for drug-related offences more than doubled in 2022 compared to 2021. Executions for drugs offences were recorded in Iran (255), Saudi Arabia (57), Singapore (11) and China, and amounted to 37% of total executions recorded globally by Amnesty. Executions for drug-related offences were also likely to have been carried out in Vietnam, yet these figures remain a state secret. Drug-related executions are in clear violation of international human rights law which states that executions should only be carried out for the 'most serious crimes' (crimes that involve intentional killing).

Positive news

Amnesty's report also charts global progress towards abolition of the death penalty. During 2022, six countries abolished the death penalty either fully or partially. Kazakhstan, Papua New Guinea, Sierra Leone and the Central African Republic abolished capital punishment for all crimes, while Equatorial Guinea and Zambia abolishing the death penalty for a certain number of crimes. Liberia and Ghana took legislative steps towards abolishing the death penalty, and the authorities in Sri Lanka and the Maldives said they would no longer resort to implementing death sentences. Bills to abolish the mandatory death penalty were also tabled in the Malaysian parliament.

16 May 2023

Debate

As a class, debate the death penalty. Half of the class will be for, and the other half, against.

Britons don't tend to support the death penalty… until you name the worst crimes

By Isabelle Kirk

The last execution in the UK took place in August 1964, and the death penalty has been abolished in the UK for over 50 years. Nevertheless, there are still numerous petitions for the government to bring back the death penalty, and YouGov data reveals many Britons support capital punishment.

Our survey shows that four in 10 (40%) Britons support the death penalty, with half (50%) opposed and 10% unsure.

Conservative voters are much more likely to support the death penalty (58% support, 34% oppose) than Labour voters (23% support, 66% oppose). Britons aged over 65 are also more than twice as likely as those aged 18-24 to back the death penalty, by 54% to 22%.

Conservative voters and older Britons are more likely to support the death penalty

Generally speaking, do you support or oppose the death penalty?

■ Strongly support　■ Tend to support　▨ Don't know　■ Tend to oppose　■ Strongly oppose

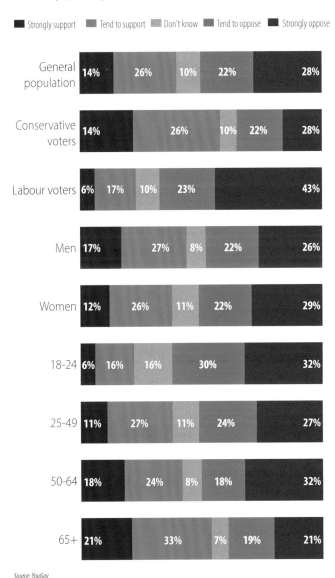

	Strongly support	Tend to support	Don't know	Tend to oppose	Strongly oppose
General population	14%	26%	10%	22%	28%
Conservative voters	14%	26%	10%	22%	28%
Labour voters	6%	17%	10%	23%	43%
Men	17%	27%	8%	22%	26%
Women	12%	26%	11%	22%	29%
18-24	6%	16%	16%	30%	32%
25-49	11%	27%	11%	24%	27%
50-64	18%	24%	8%	18%	32%
65+	21%	33%	7%	19%	21%

Source: YouGov

Britons are more likely than not to support the death penalty for the worst crimes, but not for all cases of murder

Should the death penalty be reintroduced for…?

■ Would support the death penalty for this　▨ Don't know　■ Would oppose the death penalty for this

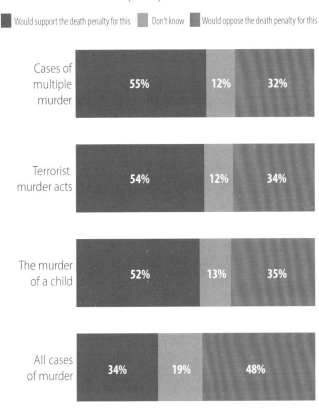

	Would support the death penalty for this	Don't know	Would oppose the death penalty for this
Cases of multiple murder	55%	12%	32%
Terrorist murder acts	54%	12%	34%
The murder of a child	52%	13%	35%
All cases of murder	34%	19%	48%

Source: YouGov

Men are slightly more likely than women to support the death penalty, by 44% to 39%, but women are no more or less likely to oppose the death penalty than men (51% of women oppose, compared to 48% of men, which is within margin of error).

However, when asked about the death penalty for specific crimes, Britons are more likely than not to support the death penalty for the murder of a child, murders committed as part of a terrorist act and cases of multiple murder. They do not, however, support the death penalty being applied to all cases of murder.

30 March 2022

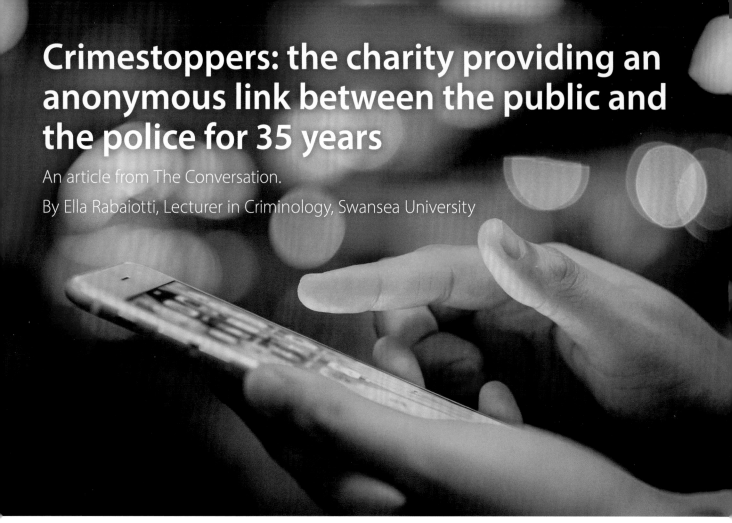

Crimestoppers: the charity providing an anonymous link between the public and the police for 35 years

An article from The Conversation.

By Ella Rabaiotti, Lecturer in Criminology, Swansea University

Crimestoppers, the crime-fighting charity, has been an anonymous link between the UK public and the police for 35 years. From everyday concerns about drug dealing and dangerous driving to taking critical information on murders, Crimestoppers receives more than half a million reports each year.

But despite its ongoing success, there has been very little research into the inner workings of the charity. My own study found the anonymity offered by Crimestoppers enables people to come forward with information about violent or organised crime. In fact, this can be more of a motivating factor than a reward.

Originating in the US in the mid-1970s and replicated across the globe, Crimestoppers programmes often offer cash rewards for tip offs. The UK charity was originally established as the Community Action Trust in 1988.

It was largely in response to the death of PC Keith Blakelock during the Broadwater Farm estate riots in London in 1985. At the time, police said that someone knew who was responsible for his murder, but were too afraid to come forward.

While in England Crimestoppers was set up to address community mistrust and loss of confidence in policing, it was advertised differently across the rest of the UK. In Northern Ireland, residents were told to phone 'without fear and without involvement'. And in Wales and Scotland,

Crimestoppers has been framed as a friendly community service.

Embracing television reconstructions has been critical to the growth of Crimestoppers across the world. Research suggests that media appeals in general can assist with solving crime in a small number of the most serious cases.

Contributions from appeals for information are thought to have helped bring some notorious criminals to justice. Serial killer, Peter Moore, came to the police's attention in 1995, following an anonymous tip off.

And a Crimestoppers reward was offered for a violent robbery carried out by John Cooper in 1996. In 2011, he was eventually convicted of murdering four people in Pembrokeshire, Wales, as well as many other serious offences. Evidence from a string of burglaries and robberies had led police to suspect he was responsible for more serious crimes.

However, the extent of Crimestoppers' support in solving such crimes is largely unknown due to the organisation's guaranteed promise of anonymity. A study by the Home Office 20 years ago outlined the benefits of the UK scheme, showing 17% of actionable information resulted in an arrest.

Nowadays, some insight is detailed in Crimestoppers' annual reports which include outcomes of awareness campaigns and 'most wanted' appeals.

During the course of my research, I discovered the charity has a strong relationship with the police, unlike the people who contact Crimestoppers.

Due to being unable to speak to anonymous callers themselves, I interviewed contact centre staff to gather their views and experiences. I also spoke with police officers who deal with Crimestoppers reports, as well as community-based officers who are often faced with people unwilling to report crime.

Participants suggested perceptions of fear and injustice impact on whether crimes are reported, especially in some close-knit communities. For example, a neighbourhood officer told me that sometimes generations of people are unlikely to go to the police, including members of his own family:

My grandmother, she's the font of knowledge in the village where she lives, she wouldn't be going to the police as a first port of call.

An independent policing review last year found that public confidence in the police has declined while the fear of crime continues to be a rising concern.

This is particularly true for those living in deprived areas and for people from minority ethnic backgrounds. Crimestoppers' own survey also suggests those groups are the most likely to contact them.

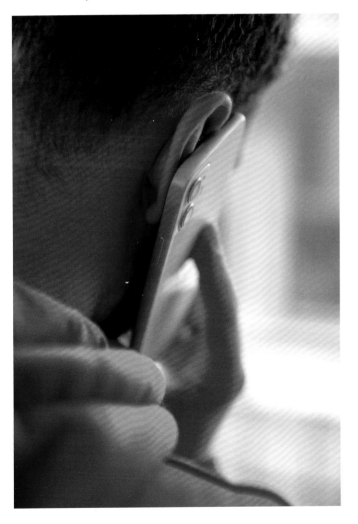

The digital age

One of the biggest changes over the past 35 years has been the move to online crime reporting. According to its own figures, Crimestoppers states 75% of information passed to the police now comes via its website.

There are often confidential police helplines for specific crimes (for example, domestic violence and hate crime), but Crimestoppers remains the primary anonymous crime reporting mechanism. One study suggests Crimestoppers supports crowdsourcing of so-called 'collective intelligence' through social networks, and this acts as a driver to online reporting.

In 2019, Crimestoppers was criticised for using cookies on its website, which allow for users to be tracked. But the charity maintained that it does not monitor individuals either online or offline.

Rewards

It also remains unclear whether Crimestoppers' offer of cash rewards has stood the test of time. My research has mirrored previous studies demonstrating that while police officers see a use in rewards, their availability is a motivating factor in only a minority of cases.

Perhaps the greatest value of rewards is in raising public interest within a busy media landscape. Crimestoppers recently offered its biggest reward of £200,000 in connection with the murder of Olivia Pratt-Korbel, the 9-year old girl who was shot in Liverpool in September 2022.

Ultimately though, it is the reassurance offered by Crimestoppers' anonymity guarantee and fuss-free participation which supports people in making reports, and enables the police to receive information they may otherwise have not received.

2 May 2023

> ### Design
>
> Design a poster for Crimestoppers or Fearless, the dedicated youth service from Crimestoppers.
>
> Include their contact information and their social media.

THE CONVERSATION

The above information is reprinted with kind permission from The Conversation.
© 2010-2024, The Conversation Trust (UK) Limited
www.theconversation.com

Useful Websites

Useful Websites

www.actionforraceequality.org.uk

www.amnesty.org.uk

www.fullfact.org

www.gov.uk

www.heraldscotland.com

www.includeyouth.org

www.independent.co.uk

www.law.ac.uk

www.lawdit.co.uk

www.lawstuff.org.uk

www.metro.co.uk

www.parliament.uk

www.politicshome.com

www.revisesociology.com

www.rocketlawyer.com

www.theconversation.com

www.theguardian.com

www.yougov.co.uk

Where can I find help?

Below are some telephone numbers, email addresses and websites of agencies or charities that can offer support or advice if you, or someone you know, needs it.

Action Fraud
Tel: 0300 123 2040
www.actionfraud.police.uk

Catch 22
Tel: 020 7336 4800
www.catch-22.org.uk

Crimestoppers
Tel: 0800 555 111
www.crimestoppers-uk.org

National Crime Agency
Tel: 0370 496 7622
www.nationalcrimeagency.gov.uk

Restorative Justice Council
www.restorativejustice.org.uk

The Ben Kinsella Trust
www.benkinsella.org.uk

Victim Support
Supportline: 08 08 16 89 111
www.victimsupport.org.uk

Victim Support Scotland
Support helpline: 0800 160 1985
www.victimsupport.scot

Why Me?
Tel: 020 3096 7708
www.why-me.org

In an emergency always call 999.

To report non-urgent crime please call your local police on 101. You can also report crime anonymously to Crimestoppers by calling 0800 555 111 or by visiting www.crimestoppers-uk.org

Glossary

BAME

An acronym which stands for Black, Asian and Minority Ethnic backgrounds.

Barrister

A barrister pleads the case on behalf of the client and the client's solicitor.

CEOP

Child Exploitation and Online Protection – CEOP is a law enforcement agency and is there to help keep children and young people safe from sexual abuse and grooming online.

Coroner

A doctor or lawyer responsible for investigating deaths.

Counter-terrorism

Counter-terrorism refers to the tactics and techniques used by governments and other groups to prevent or minimise a terrorist threat.

County lines

'County lines' is a term used to describe criminal gangs from big cities who expand their operations to smaller towns. They groom and exploit children and vulnerable people to traffick and sell drugs for them.

Crime

Crime may be defined as an act or omission prohibited or punished by law. A 'criminal offence' includes any infringement of the criminal law, from homicide to riding a bicycle without lights. What is classified as a crime is supposed to reflect the values of society and to reinforce those values. If an act is regarded as harmful to society or its citizens, it is often, but not always, classified as a criminal offence.

Crime Survey for England & Wales (CSEW)

The Crime Survey for England and Wales (CSEW) is an organised study of national crime trends. It measures the levels and types of crime in England and Wales by asking people about whether they or members of their households have experienced any crimes in the past year.

Criminal Justice System (CJS)

The Criminal Justice System is the set of agencies and processes established by governments to control crime and impose penalties on those who violate law.

Crown Court

The Crown Court deals with the most serious criminal offences. Usually with a jury who decide the verdict, and a judge who passes the sentence (punishment).

Cybercrime

Crime with some kind of 'computer' or 'cyber' aspect to it: using modern telecommunication networks such as the Internet (like chat rooms, e-mails and forums) and mobile phones (texting) to intentionally psychically or mentally harm and cause distress. Computer viruses, cyberstalking, identity theft and phishing scams are some examples of cybercrime.

Deterrent

Any threat or punishment which is seen to deter someone from a certain action: the threat of prison, for example, is expected to function as a deterrent to criminal behaviour.

Ethnic minority

A group of people who are different in their ancestry, culture and traditions from the majority of the population.

Fraud

The act of deceiving or conning someone for financial gain.

Judge

A judge is the person in a court of law who decides how the law should be applied, for example how criminals should be punished.

Jury

A jury consists on twelve members of the public who are called upon to consider evidence provided to them in court and decide upon a verdict.

Magistrate

Magistrates, also known as Justices of the Peace, are individuals from all walks of life who are passionate about making a difference in their local communities. Almost anyone can become a magistrate, you do not need formal qualifications or legal training to become a magistrate.

Magistrates' court

All criminal cases start in a magistrates' court. Cases are heard by either, 2 or 3 magistrates, or a district judge. There is not a jury in a magistrates' court.

Peer/youth court

An alternative approach to sentencing for young people. In the peer/youth court system, a young person who is charged with a crime appears in front of a jury of their peers for sentencing. The person being charged must agree to take part in the process.

Index